RICH BRAIN, POOR BRAIN

Bridging Social and Synaptic Gaps in Schools

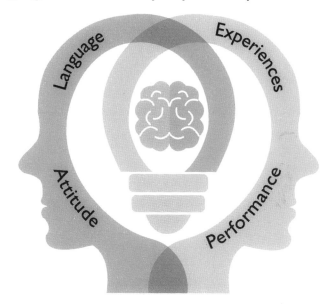

Language · Experiences · Attitude · Performance

Written by Dr. Linda Karges-Bone

Edited by Bonnie Krueger
Cover and book design by Patti Jeffers

ISBN 978-0-7877-2510-5

P.O. Box 802 • Dayton, OH 45401-0802 • www.LorenzEducationalPress.com

Dedication

For Carolyn, Audrey, and Katie, my first and best students, and now J.D., Ph.D. and Ph.D. – all the products of public education. I guess it worked.

With thanks To Mr. Geoff Lorenz, owner and publisher of Lorenz Educational Press, a man who has a vision for a better world for all children.

With gratitude and respect to my voices from the field:

Dirk Bedford, Rick Blanchard, Johnnie Boatwright, Rick Brewer, Luci Carter, Don Clerico, Dana Clerico Hedgepeth, Andre Dukes, Lisa Hendricks, Amanda Hobson Barnett, LaDene Conroy, Priscilla Johnson, Jack O'Connor, Camacia Smith-Ross, and Ann M. Watson

Message to Teachers, Principals, and Parents

Unless you have struggled to give a child everything, against all odds and in spite of what the culture, economic climate, and the community around you say that you are *allowed* to have, you will not appreciate this book. Your children have the right to a full and robust education in a land of plenty. It will not be easy to achieve, but if you are reading this book, you already know that.

Do not give up. Do not give in. Press on.

Whatever course you decide upon, there is always someone to tell you that you are wrong. There are always difficulties arising which tempt you to believe that your critics are right. To map out a course of action and follow it to an end requires courage. – Ralph Waldo Emerson

Don't be discouraged. It's often the last key in the bunch that opens the lock. – Anonymous

Table of Contents

No person, I think, ever saw a herd of buffalo, of which a few were fat and the great majority lean. No person ever saw a flock of birds, of which two or three were swimming in grease, and the others all skin and bone.
                  – Henry George, American political economist

Introduction

The causes which destroyed the ancient republics were numerous; but in Rome, one principal cause was the vast inequality of fortunes.
          — Noah Webster, American editor and writer

When I was a doctoral candidate in the early 1990's, I spent many hours debating (in written and oral formats) the tensions between equity and equality. It was and is an argument with no reconciliation, only an endless series of questions and challenges. I have spent most of my career as a professor, author, speaker and media host exploring these questions and challenges:

- Why do some schools have so much, and others so little?
- What does it mean to be a wealthy, or "rich," school?
- What makes a school "poor"?
- Is it *always* about money?
- Is it *only* about money?
- Should we be trying to make everything the same for all students?
- Can we try something different?

What does the research in cognitive science tell us about children's brains that can answer all of the questions above?

Rich Brain, Poor Brain is a book that explores the differences that separate students' opportunities for success in American schools. We know that poverty is the great separator, the distinction, the threat. In the beginning, we will discuss the research on the threats of poverty to teachers, students, and communities. We will consider some fresh insights about ways that poverty shapes brains and behaviors. Then we will explore ways to change outcomes for students who live in poverty or those who attend schools that are not enriched to the extent that they challenge all children.

An Important Proviso

Poverty is no joke. It cannot be minimalized, marginalized, or truly understood by anyone who has never "done without" for any length of time. The constant pressures of never having enough to pay the bills, to get ahead, to go to the doctor or dentist for anything other than a life-threatening event or to feel full and satisfied after a meal wear an individual, a family and ultimately a community down. As I write this book, our local paper, the *Charleston Post and Courier*, is wrapping up a well-crafted series about high-poverty neighborhood schools devastated by social and economic change. Describing an inner city school that has sadly become a typical prototype, the reporter writes:

> Many students at North Charleston High have faced near homelessness, street violence, severe family instability or other major upheavals in their young lives. Although the campus sits right off Park Circle, one of the region's trendiest spots, Spruill Avenue has become the main street for many left here. It's a high-crime stretch beyond the reach of gentrification where windows hide behind boards and bars, porches sag and generations live mired in minimum wage poverty. That's because the school, which should house a diverse group of 1,141 students from across its attendance zone, instead enrolled just 450 this year — and shrinking. Nearly 90 percent of its students are black in an area that's more than a quarter white, and virtually all left are poor." This series describes, in poignant and honest detail, the plight of many high poverty, Title I schools in our country, "left behind", inadvertently, but still, by the government, by parents seeking better opportunities for their children, and by communities that do not understand the needs of our students across diverse social and learning continuums. (Berry-Hawes, 2015)

Rich Brain, Poor Brain: Bridging Social and Synaptic Gaps in Schools is not the answer to large, amorphous, porous educational questions. It is, however, a conversation about possibilities. It is one step in a long journey that will, I believe, have many waypoints. Every community will have to explore ways to make public schools work for them. It seems that one keyword to meeting needs and responding to shifts in social and economic pressures is *choice*. School choice, vouchers, AP academies, junior first grade, expanded Head Start, reading and literacy coaches, arts-focused schools – the list goes on and on. Choice is the life-blood. This book is about simple choices that any site can make. You do not need legislation, representation or much deliberation to implement one or all of the choices in *Rich Brain, Poor Brain*. You simply need to believe that the threats of poverty can, with careful planning and innovation, be minimized so that learning can occur with greater ease.

> *Rich Brain, Poor Brain: Bridging Social and Synaptic Gaps in Schools* is not the answer to large, amorphous, porous educational questions. It is, however, a conversation about possibilities.

It is important to note that many high-poverty or Title I sites are doing amazing work already. Indeed, part of the reason I am writing this book is to honor their work and to spread the word that an excellent education can be offered to all students when creativity and commitment to high expectations are set free. Still there are, as we will see in subsequent pages, huge and ugly gaps in access to quality schools and education.

This section will define and outline the impact of poverty on learning and socialization, and then compare differences between the opportunities that "rich brains" and "poor brains" are given in ordinary academic settings. In particular, we will consider inequities and accompanying solutions to the social and synaptic gaps that impact schools and education across four broad areas:

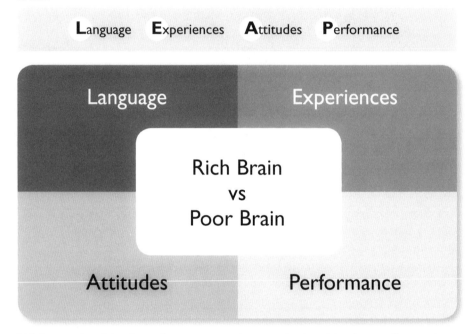

Language   Experiences   Attitudes   Performance

Language

Experiences

Rich Brain
vs
Poor Brain

Attitudes

Performance

Within each of the four dynamics, teachers and school leaders will consider the research and big ideas behind the gaps that exist between "rich brains" and "poor brains" but take it an innovative, and perhaps a bit risky, step further. As the acronym suggests, this book will help schools to LEAP across gaps. Under each of the four areas, there will be three strategies, programming recommendations or big ideas that can be implemented in Title I or high-poverty sites, or indeed any site, with relative ease and modest cost. In the vernacular, we will attempt a high-quality "knockoff" of the designer brand.

Money isn't always the answer. Yes, there will be some expense associated with these ideas and strategies, but not much. I will not recommend a single program or a brand. These "knockoffs" of designer academia are largely teacher-generated, home-grown, and simple. Often they are rooted in old-fashioned, organic pedagogy that we have put aside as less fashionable.

As always, things come around, only now we have the brain research to legitimize them.

Please forgive the humor associated with this "knockoff" vernacular. When I think of the best and most innovative teachers and leaders whom I have encountered in public education, their sense of humor and positive outlook are what I remember most and have proven to be part of what serves them best.

Moving forward, as we LEAP across social and synaptic gaps posed by poverty and the accompanying threats, we will deal with issues such as literacy, critical thinking, and global studies as they are experienced in a wealthy school setting as well as in a high-poverty setting. We will then examine how high-poverty sites can borrow and re-purpose ideas from "rich brain" sites to make them accessible and available in "poor brain" sites (or indeed in any school that wants to do more with fewer assets). Ultimately these strategies will find a home where any leader wants to implement creative, flexible, and interesting ways to teach and learn.

> There is nothing funny about poverty. However, as one who emerged from a culture of "have nots" where girls were not encouraged to do more than take a secretarial course and look for a husband, and from a family where I was expected to work hard from the age of 16 and there was no money for further education, I learned quickly that a sense of humor is a powerful tonic and a way to break down social and emotional barriers.

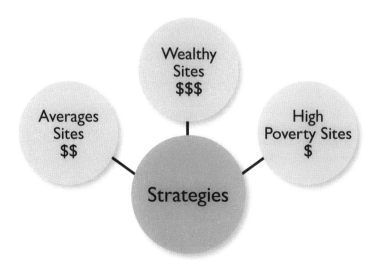

Remember, the terms *rich brain* and *poor brain* are not meant to be disparaging, pejorative, or a judgment concerning individuals or communities, but a stark and simple label for inequities that hold back social progress. Knowing this, school leaders, parents, teachers and communities can make better, more informed choices about the programs and curricula that they want in their sites. To that end, let's begin with a look at how rich-brain and poor-brain sites describe themselves on the front pages of their school websites. In the following table, consider descriptive language about the school, vision, curriculum, and programming taken from a variety of school media pages. Can you see, hear, and feel the differences in tone and intent? Which schools would you want your child or grandchild to attend?

> Remember, the terms *rich brain* and *poor brain* are not meant to be disparaging, pejorative, or a judgment concerning individuals or communities, but a stark and simple label for inequities that hold back social progress.

Front (Web) Page News

Rich Brain School	Poor Brain School	Your Thoughts?
"Inquisitive and independent projects"	"Come to school every day ready to learn"	
"Transformative experience"	"Think bigger"	
Focus on new mosaic or artwork in the site	Focus on bus safety	
"Competitive"	"High standards"	
Video of field day or thank-you tea for volunteers	Links to test scores	
"Upper school and lower school" "Academy"	"Grade levels" "Classrooms"	
"Maximizing creativity"	"Maximizing respect"	

Remember what the philosopher Stephen Covey said? "Perception IS reality." What might happen if we see poor schools from a different perspective? From behind a different filter? This is what we call a *paradigm shift*.

> *The word* paradigm *comes from the Greek. It was originally a scientific term, and is more commonly used today to mean a model, theory, perception, assumption, or frame of reference. In the more general sense, it's the way we "see" the world — not in terms of our visual sense of sight, but in terms of perceiving, understanding, and interpreting. We interpret everything we experience through these mental maps. We seldom question their accuracy; we're usually even unaware that we have them. We simply assume that the way we see things is the way they really are or the way they should be.* (Covey, 1989)

Rich Brain, Poor Brain is not an antidote. It is a tonic. It is a way to do more with what one has or with what one can get in an ordinary school setting. It is, as Covey suggested, about making a new mental map. This book is not intended for political persuasion, and indeed, may not always be deemed politically correct. Some of the voices and choices in this book may provoke criticism and discussion. This can be a good thing if it helps to move all children forward.

In closing, the strategies presented across the four paradigms of LEAP are not extraordinary, but their impact might be.

Voices from the Field

Each chapter will contain research, strategies, and perhaps most importantly, *Voices from the Field*, the opinions and reflections from a dozen or more teachers, Title I leaders, professors and community activists who have examined the ideas in *Rich Brain, Poor Brain* and think they are worthy of implementation. Their words will inspire you.

Chapter One ● ● ● ● ● ● ● ●

The Threats and Implications of Poverty: Painful, Powerful, and Pervasive

The mother's battle for her child with sickness, with poverty, with war, with all the forces of exploitation and callousness that cheapen human life needs to become a common human battle, waged in love and in the passion for survival.

— Adrienne Rich

How pervasive is poverty in America today? The latest U.S. census data tells the sad story in numbers too powerful to ignore:

In 2013, approximately 21 percent of school-age children were in families living in poverty. The percentage of school-age children living in poverty ranged across the United States from 9 percent in New Hampshire to 33 percent in Mississippi. — U.S. Census Bureau

Roughly one in five children under the age of 18 lives in poverty, a situation defined by the U.S. Census Bureau using economic data to determine the amount of income needed to maintain basic needs. To give you an idea of what this means, the chart below shows poverty thresholds as of September 2015.

Persons In Household	Poverty Threshold in Dollars
1	$11,770
2	$15,930
3	$20,090
4	$24,250
5	$28,410
6	$32,570
7	$36,730

Source: U.S. Census Bureau

Moreover, poverty in the U.S. seems to be more prevalent in non-white populations. As the table below demonstrates, black, Hispanic and American Indian/Alaska Native populations are represented at two-to-three times the rate of white or Asian groups.

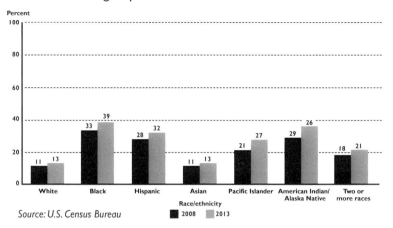

Source: U.S. Census Bureau

Consistent with these trends, we find that geographic regions of our country that are home to larger minority populations will also suffer from the impact of poverty on schools. In both non-metro (rural or suburban) and metro (urban) areas of the south and west, poverty rates are significantly higher than in other regions.

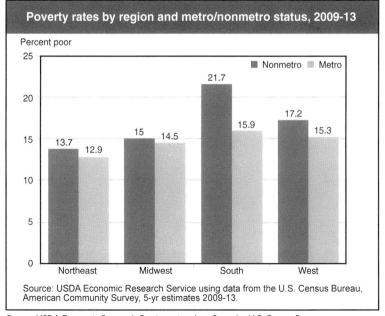

Source: USDA Economic Research Service using data from the U.S. Census Bureau

Poverty is certainly everywhere, especially when one factors in the working poor, that enormous and rapidly growing group of American families who do not meet federal guidelines for assistance but who can barely make it on what they earn. Recently, I volunteered with my university students at a food distribution project in a suburban community. Amid the pastoral, seemingly healthy setting, we met hundreds lining up for monthly help with food staples. Nearly everyone was working, more than one job in fact, but trends in employment that preclude full-time wages and accompanying benefits have left millions of families on the edge of disaster any given month. The strategies in this book will be especially useful in sites that serve populations of the working poor with few extra resources for programming and interventions.

And poverty is persistent. It is generational. It will neither give in nor give up as it gnaws away at families and the schools that their children and grandchildren attend. The image below depicts clusters of counties in the United States that have held stubbornly to high child poverty rates for decades.

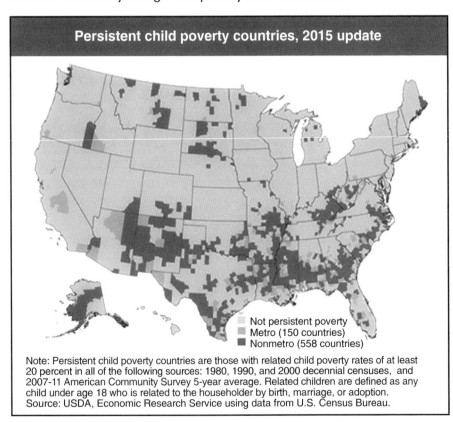

Persistent child poverty countries, 2015 update

- Not persistent poverty
- Metro (150 countries)
- Nonmetro (558 countries)

Note: Persistent child poverty countries are those with related child poverty rates of at least 20 percent in all of the following sources: 1980, 1990, and 2000 decennial censuses, and 2007-11 American Community Survey 5-year average. Related children are defined as any child under age 18 who is related to the householder by birth, marriage, or adoption.
Source: USDA, Economic Research Service using data from U.S. Census Bureau.

Source: U.S. Department of Agriculture Economic Research Service

Again we see clusters, and in these clusters are the schools that desperately need infusions of energy and creative strategies. It is for these schools especially that *Rich Brain, Poor Brain* will have meaning. There is no single answer for helping children move out of generational poverty, but that is no excuse to give up trying.

Dr. Ruby K. Payne has certainly never given up. Her essential book, *Frameworks of Poverty*, is considered by many who work in high-poverty schools to be a critical tool in understanding the challenges that face families, and subsequently, their children's schools and teachers. Dr. Payne is a leading expert on the mindsets of socioeconomic classes and poverty education. According to her website, the book provides "a foundation for understanding the hidden rules of poverty, middle class, and wealth, and offers strategies to address the impact of poverty on people's lives."

Understanding the distinct variations among social classes is a first step in considering the application of strategies found in this book. Perhaps one of the most helpful discussions as it pertains to the ideas in *Rich Brain, Poor Brain* is the hidden rules among classes. According to Dr. Payne, the "hidden rules" are those tacit, private, and cultural directives learned and passed on about how to behave, place value, and commit time and energy. I will discuss three of the hidden rules that seem most enlightening when understanding the disparities between rich-brain and poor-brain schools. These are values concerning time, education, and ultimately, destiny. (Payne, 2008)

Time

- Poor families believe that time operates on a continuum in which the PRESENT is most important, and decisions are made based on feelings and survival.

- Middle-class families believe that time operates on a continuum in which the FUTURE is most important, and decisions are made with the future in mind.

- Wealthy families focus time on traditions and history, and decisions reflect the need for decorum.

Reflection: How can we implement strategies that persuade children and families living in poverty that their time is worth spending on education, when it has not traditionally been available or paid off in terms of immediate returns?

Education

- Poor families value education, but in the abstract.

- Middle-class families see education as crucial, necessary for making money and achieving goals.

- Wealthy families regard education as a given, a tradition that serves to build and maintain connections.

Destiny

This brings us to destiny, that deep, underlying belief system about where we will ultimately end up, what the fates will allow, what is possible and probable, and what we should even attempt to do.

- For poor families, destiny is about fate and chance. There is not much we can do to change life's path, and therefore it is probably not worth trying to change.

- For middle-class families, the keyword is *choice*. Make good choices, and you will channel your future for the better.

- As for wealthy families, destiny is just your path in life, to do well and be well. It would be a great surprise if this wasn't the case.

Moving through chapters four, five and six, you may notice the impact of Ruby Payne's work as the strategies focus on both cognitive and affective domains of learning. There is also a deep commitment to *social learning*, the process in which individuals observe the behavior of others and its consequences, and modify their own behavior accordingly.

During childhood, children acquire language, attitudes, behaviors and beliefs that shape their eventual trajectories through life. This is a lovely thing, as long as those early experiences do not limit the paths or potential of the children. Poverty does that. It sets limits. How? Follow this timeline from increased cortisol levels to sabotaging personal potential.

Poverty Triggers cortisol, the stress hormone	**Cortisol** Shrinks the hippocampus and impedes neurogenesis, harming brain development	**Harm to the Brain** Slows down language, reduces creativity, and sabotages potential

How seriously should we take the threats of stress, whether due to poverty alone or to the myriad of accompanying factors such as abuse and neglect that so often present concurrently? The answer may be in epigenetics, according to Dr. Seth Pollak and a team of researchers at the University of Wisconsin. Stress, like the chronic stress of childhood poverty, can permanently alter the brain by attacking the outside of the genes (hence the term *epigenetic*). It has to do with NR3C1, a protein-coding gene that senses the hormone cortisol.

NR3C1 is a protein-coding gene that senses the hormone cortisol. It may be the key to understanding epigenetic changes attributable to poverty.

> *"We know about these difficulties, but we've had a really hard time understanding why. What's getting under people's skin?" Pollak says. "Why are they still having the social difficulties and the emotional difficulties because of something that happened when they were two?" Increasingly, scientists are coming to realize that people's experiences exert a strong influence on their biology by silencing genes or turning them back on, significantly changing the way a cell functions without changing its DNA sequence. It's a phenomenon known as epigenetics. "Epigenetics makes the genes tick," explains Moshe Szyf, a professor of genetics and pharmacology at McGill University. "Epigenetic changes modify DNA to keep genes from being expressed, and they can explain dramatic differences between cells with identical DNA—for example, how stem cells can turn into either liver cells or heart cells, or why only one of a set of identical twins gets cancer. It's also, Pollak found, why children who grow up in abusive homes have physical and psychological problems that haunt them well into adulthood." (Nelsen, 2014)*

In high-poverty schools, where cortisol is constantly attacking brain development and daily performance, students need fresh interventions that will hopefully "re-thicken" the cortex that has been thinned by the persistent, unrelenting seepage of stress hormones. As one researcher posits, cortisol acts like battery acid on the brain. What effects might you see? In my book *Differentiated Pathways of the Brain*, I look at ways that boys and girls might react to pervasive stress. (Karges-Bone, 2010)

Stress Reactions in Children

Boys' Brains	Girls' Brains
Aggression	Eating disorders
Bullying	Self-harming (cutting)
Withdrawal	Self-criticism
Sexual aggression	Promiscuity
Cursing, tough language, threats	Cursing, tough language, drama
Taking on adult roles by stealing or dealing drugs to make money for the family	Taking on adult roles by caring for siblings

Another Important Voice on Families and Poverty

Another important voice that fuels my desire to find ways to help teachers in high-poverty sites is that of sociologist Dr. Annette Lareau. Her book *Unequal Childhoods: Class, Race, and Family Life*, published in 2003, offers a fascinating glimpse into the differences among families that seem to stem from their economic circumstances. Having money, especially having enough money, over generations shapes the ways that families look at schools and schooling. These differences are important to understand and factor in when teaching in high-poverty sites.

On her university web-page, Dr. Lareau outlines her work:

> *How does social stratification have an impact on life chances? Americans believe in the power of the individual to shape his or her life prospects. In my research, I have sought to unpack how social structural forces do, and do not, shape crucial aspects of daily life. My book, Unequal Childhoods: Class, Race, and Family Life is based on participant-observation of a total of twelve*

white and African-American families with children in third and fourth grade. The work suggests that all parents want their children to be healthy and happy. Middle-class parents, however, see their children as a project. They seek to develop their talents and skills through a series of organized activities, through an intensive process of reasoning and language development, and through close supervision of their experiences in school. By contrast, working-class and poor families work hard to feed, clothe, and protect their children. But they also presume that their children will spontaneously grow and thrive. Thus the children "hang out" by watching television and playing with cousins rather than being in organized activities, are given directives rather than being engaged in reasoning, and are given independence in schools and other institutions. Although African-American families live in racially segregated neighborhoods and experience racial discrimination in employment, in the kinds of child rearing practices examined in this study, the white and African-American upper-middle-class are extremely similar in their child rearing practices. There is a significant difference between the working-class and middle-class African-American families. (http://sociology.sas.upenn.edu/ annette_lareau)

In *Rich Brain, Poor Brain* we will consider specific strategies for use in lesson design, curriculum implementation, school climate and culture, and classroom management. These strategies may help shift students' thinking toward attitudes, behaviors, choices and performance on standardized tests that could help move them out of generational poverty.

Entire books, doctoral theses and political campaigns have been built upon the compelling research concerning the impact of poverty on learning. Deficits, gaps, delays, challenges… whatever words used, the outcomes are dismal. What is unique and even hopeful about the conversations we can now have concerning poverty and learning is based on emerging research on *neuroplasticity*, the brain's ability to respond to stress, changes, injury, or attack by regrouping, recharging and reconfiguring neural pathways to survive and thrive.

Even though the latest studies suggest that the income gap is feeding a cognition gap, actual, measurable differences between the prefrontal cortexes of low-income and middle-class children, there is also concurrent research affirming the radical abilities of young brains to mend themselves.

Researchers at Baylor University had already noticed that growing up in an environment that was not enriched actually resulted in a brain with less volume. But the results of this latest work, done partly at Duke University, is startling, and contributes to the mandate for changing the ways we do business in high-poverty schools:

> The influence of poverty on children's learning and achievement is mediated by structural brain development. To avoid long-term costs of impaired academic functioning, households below 150% of the federal poverty level should be targeted for additional resources aimed at remediating early childhood environments.

(Hair, 2015)

It appears that factors such as inferior or inconsistent prenatal care, poor nutrition during childhood, toxic environments, lack of early educational and literacy opportunities, and the always pervasive influence of stress on the brain take a terrible toll. Alison Gopnik, writing in her Wall Street Journal column *Mind & Matter*, summarizes it this way:

> The process of evolution has designed brains to be shaped by the outside world. That's the whole point of having one. Two complementary processes play an especially important role in this shaping. In one process, what neuroscientists call "proliferation," the brain makes many new connections between neurons. In the other process, "pruning," some existing connections get stronger, while others disappear. Experience heavily influences both proliferation and pruning.

> The important point, and the good news, is that brain plasticity never ends. Brains can be changed throughout life, and we never entirely lose the ability to learn and change. But, equally importantly, childhood is the time of the greatest opportunity, and the greatest risk. We lose the potential of millions of young American brains every day. (Gopnik, 2015)

Neuroplasticity, the unique and powerful ability to reconfigure, transform, regroup and recapture, is what makes our human brains so awesome and this book so helpful. If we can address the threats of poverty, stress and educational inequities during critical periods in childhood, there is a good chance we can help restore many children's brains to healthy, competitive levels.

> **The Clock is Ticking**
>
> This tension between proliferation and pruning is what drives the mandate for finding fresh ways to help teachers and their administrators.

But the clock is ticking. In my workshops on the brain and poverty, I ask participants to number a sheet of paper, and then create a visual that looks like this:

```
1.    NCLB = Third Grade
2.    Age 9 = Pruning
3.    4th Grade = Prison
```

"What is the relationship among these variables?" I ask.

Here's the story in a very, very simplistic way:

1. The original No Child Left Behind mandate was to have students reading on grade level by the end of third grade.

2. There was a reason for that. Brain research suggests that *neural pruning*, the removal of unused neural pathways, kicks in at around age 9. If we can't get students on a reading trajectory in time, they may lose critical pathways.

3. What happens when students cannot read on time and well enough to feel confident in school? Well, consider the fact that the average reading comprehension of those incarcerated in our prisons is roughly at the 4th-grade level. Without interventions, especially in literacy, we sentence children to a limited and often hopeless path in life.

Summary of Chapter One's Big Ideas

- Poverty is pervasive, generational, and difficult to address in schools and communities.

- Poverty informs the ways that families think about schools and schooling.

- Poverty attacks the brain by triggering the stress hormone cortisol, which affects growth, performance and function in profound ways.

- Poverty appears to change the actual thickness of the pre-frontal cortex, having a potentially disastrous effect on children's potential.

- The thickness of the pre-frontal cortex can be treated, potentially, by enrichment and interventions such as those in the LEAP model found in this book. This will work best if introduced prior to neural pruning at around age 9 or 10.

- The clock is ticking. It is only a matter of time before the threats of poverty take away the opportunities to learn and grow and find joy for another generation of children.

Voices from the Field:
Amanda Hobson Barnett

Early childhood educator, instructional coach in Title I sites, master's degree in poverty education, Harvard University

"When I took my first teaching position, at a school in South Carolina with students from both affluent families and those living in poverty, I was shocked at the disparity I saw. As I studied more about the achievement gap, it became obvious to me that our schools are not educating all children equally or appropriately. This compelled me to educate myself in order to become a more capable advocate for disadvantaged students and families. All students possess the ability to learn and achieve at high levels, no matter what neighborhood they live in. Through a great education, I believe that every single child in our country has the opportunity to rise out of poverty and find success in life. As a teacher and an instructional coach in inner-city schools from Harlem to Charleston, I have learned that there is one tenet that can make or break your success as a teacher in high-poverty schools: you must have high expectations for students' behavior, their ability to achieve academically, and for yourself as their teacher."

"To that end, I help teachers to acknowledge possible bias they may bring into their classrooms and to take steps to make sure these flawed assumptions do not lower expectations for student achievement. Teachers should treat teaching behavior like any other academic standard they are required to teach, and teach it until all students have mastered it. Just like instruction, teachers can personalize behavioral goal-setting for individual students. I recommend avoiding public behavior charts and shaming of students and focusing instead on explicitly re-teaching and modeling desired behaviors."

"Finally, it is crucial that teachers have high expectations for themselves. They must be intentional in their planning: thinking through each transition and lesson to keep students moving ahead, making sure that there is an appropriate level of rigor throughout the day. This is the key to student engagement."

Voices from the Field:
Dr. Don Clerico

Professor, former school administrator, director of a 14-year global education project connecting American teachers with rural schools In Ghana, West Africa

"Poverty has a devastating impact on education. It limits families' ability to obtain educational materials for their children. It severely restricts their ability to leave failing schools. It creates educational myopia by preventing poor families from seeing an attainable future. For families in poverty around the world, education is often not available or is so far out of reach as to be non-existent. When this is the case, what happens to the dreams that might have been, the goals never imagined, and the opportunities that will never come?"

"Wanting an education is not enough. We cannot have something simply because we want it. Many of us 'want' things we will never have. Perhaps you wanted to be a professional athlete, or be a famous actor, or musician, or politician. I always wanted to be a cowboy and ride my horse across the western prairies. But, wanting is not sufficient to having. One must first be prepared and qualified. Only then is it possible to achieve your dreams. This is why one of the primary functions of education is to prepare and qualify us so that dreams can become reality or at least a reasonable possibility. But we can only dream about those things we know about. We can only imagine ourselves in roles we are aware of. Which brings me to a second purpose of education: to open our eyes, minds, and hearts to new ideas, new experiences, new worlds – which, in turn, gives us new material for dreaming, new goals to strive for, new opportunities to pursue. What happens when education is not available to the poorest members of our world? This book is about making a quality education accessible to all children and offering a future without limits."

Chapter Two ● ● ● ● ● ● ● ●

Expecting Change: Teachers' Expectations in a Rich Brain-Poor Brain World

Intelligence without ambition is a bird without wings. – Salvador Dali

My teacher thought I was smarter than I was — so I was.

Six-year-old

Expect Change

Teachers' expectations matter. A lot. So much so that they can change the ways that brains eventually develop. It is not simply a feeling – it is a biological, emotional, and mental game changer. Teachers change brains when they change expectations.

Some of my best sources for writing, keeping up with teachers and schools, and generally taking the pulse of our educational community are found on social media. The quote from a six-year-old above has gone viral on a number of social media platforms. There is an important message here, one that resonates with the themes of *Rich Brain, Poor Brain*.

In 2003 I published an article in the *Journal of Early Childhood and Family Review* titled "Teachers: Doing Brain Surgery from the Inside Out" (Karges-Bone, 2003). In it, I discuss surgeons who operate on a single patient "from the outside in" with an entire team of experts supporting them. Everyone, from the social workers checking on the waiting family, to anesthesiologists, to nurses, radiologists and many more, monitors and assists with the entire process so that an optimum outcome is achieved. In contrast, classroom teachers, working alone and on multiple patients at a time, are charged with changing brains. They do it, too, but from the inside out. Hence, as I suggested in the article, teachers should be paid the same as neurosurgeons!

In response to this statement, I received at least half a dozen letters of fan mail, which, for a boring college professor, is pretty awesome. I am not the only one to make this point, however. Writing in her blog at *Education Week*,

Wendy Pillars says:

We are the only professionals whose job it is to physically alter a child's brain daily. I like how Judy Willis, accomplished neuroscientist-turned-teacher, refers to a teacher's work as a form of "bloodless brain surgery."

Here's how it happens at a basic level:
* *If a child takes in information through her sensory pathways and her brain makes the decision to keep that knowledge, the integrative process takes over and makes sense out of that learning as she sleeps.*

* *This consolidation occurs when neurons transmit messages to one another. The messages must cross microscopic chasms between the neurons—laboriously at first, and then more quickly with each subsequent moment of access.*

* *Eventually the learning is connected to several points within a denser and denser web of neurons, easing the information retrieval process for the conscious learner. As teachers, we must understand that a neural pathway is like a new path in the woods. The more frequently that a neural pathway is traveled, the fewer the obstacles, the greater its capacity, and the smoother and faster it becomes.*

But for this neuroplasticity to take hold, for teachers to be able to change brains and therefore outcomes, they must believe in their power to do so. Understanding how and why teachers who might embrace the strategies in *Rich Brain, Poor Brain* can be effective requires a step back in time to the famous Rosenthal Studies on Expectancy, or what many refer to as "self-fulfilling prophecies in the classroom." Here is what one psychology site tells us about this profound study and the subsequent impact on teachers and teaching:

What did Rosenthal and Jacobson Do?
Rosenthal and Jacobson tested children at Oak School with an IQ test, the Tests of General Ability (TOGA) at the beginning of the school year. This test was used because teachers were likely to be unfamiliar with it, and because it is primarily non-verbal, and not dependent on skills learned in school (i.e., reading and writing). In order to create an expectancy, the teachers were informed that the test was the "Harvard Test of Inflected Acquisition," which served as a measure of academic "blooming." Therefore, teachers were led to believe that certain students were entering a year of high achievement, and other students were not. In reality, the test had no such predictive validity.

Eighteen teachers at the school were informed of the students in their classes who had obtained scores in the top 20% of this test. These students were ready to realize their potential, according to their test scores. What the teachers didn't know is that students were placed on these lists completely at random. There was no difference between these students and other students whose names were not on the lists. At the end of the school year, all students were once again tested with the same test (the TOGA). In this way, the change in IQ could be estimated. Differences in the size of the changes for experimental and control group children could serve as an index of any expectancy effect.

What Can We Learn?

Rosenthal and Jacobson's results demonstrated expectancy effects. There was a marked difference in IQ test score gains. Students who had been labeled as "ready to bloom" showed greater gains than those who had not been labeled in this way. One interesting qualification to these results was that they occurred only for the youngest children (1st and 2nd graders). No consistent difference in IQ scores was observed in older children. The authors offer a number of reasons for this age difference in expectancy effects. Perhaps younger children are more changeable because of their tender age, or were perceived as more malleable by their teachers. Another possible reason for the age difference was that perhaps younger children are more susceptible to the subtle influences that are characteristic of expectation effects. (University of Wisconsin, Madison, Lecture Elaboration, http://psych.wisc.edu/braun/281/Intelligence/LabellingEffects.htm)

> **Ready or Not?**
> Rosenthal and Jacobson's results demonstrated expectancy effects. There was a marked difference in IQ test score gains. Students who had been labeled as "ready to bloom" showed greater gains than those who had not been labeled in this way.

Teachers' expectations are enormously impactful. Moreover, the greater impact on younger brains is consistent with what we now know about neural pruning and neuroplasticity. Preparing teachers to "teach to the best brain" is central to the message of this book.

Why Does It Matter So Much?

The Rosenthal and Jacobson studies on what has become known as a self-fulfilling prophecy are essential to understanding how and why so many students become trapped in a downward spiral in schools. Remember Ruby Payne's hidden rules? Look at the logic model at the top of the next page.

IF teachers in high-poverty schools believe that their students cannot be expected to do much;

AND students and parents in high-poverty zones believe in a destiny where they cannot expect much;

THEN it follows that expectations will be low on all sides and little change will occur among any of the stakeholders.

Expectations are Everything

In this paradigm, someone has to call foul and break the cycle. Because, by virtue of their educations and their missions, teachers hold more power than most parents and students. I suggest that teachers make the first move.

Dirk Bedford is the principal of the Meeting Street Academy in Charleston, South Carolina, a unique private school that serves an exclusive population of high-poverty students. Mr. Bedford relies heavily on a model in which highly motivated teachers consistently teach both behavior and academics. During a recent tour of his site in the inner city, Principal Bedford explained the 4 Pillars of the MSA model, with special emphasis on how a "transformational school experience" is constructed. In this model, Bedford shares his respect for the role of an excellent, highly qualified, fully empowered teacher.

A Four-Piece Puzzle

1	**2**	**3**	**4**
Early Education	Family Partnership	Holistic Approach	Teacher Excellence
Students begin their schooling with us as three and four year olds in a program that encourages the development of social, emotional, intellectual, and physical skills.	MSA families commit to supporting their children's education through collaborating with teachers, volunteering in the school and attending numerous family education workshops and events. MSA is dedicated to fostering the education of the entire family.	To meet the needs of the whole student, we operate on an extended day and a year-round calendar; provide medical and dental screening; and provide healthy meals and ample time for exercise.	We hire exceptional teachers and support them through embedded professional development that includes specialized training, dynamic coaching, leadership opportunities, and rewards for excellence.

Clearly all four pillars are essential, and some of them will be expensive and difficult to implement without financial underpinning. However, the Teacher Excellence pillar is my target in this chapter. Many schools across all economic and social strata can do a better job of finding, equipping, and empowering high-quality teachers. But why isn't it happening? I believe that programs and systems have overtaken our good sense and we are not allowing teachers to operate as highly qualified professionals.

Reading this section, you might be thinking that I am placing too much emphasis on teachers. How much can one teacher realistically accomplish? How real is this idea of setting expectations for children and then seeing powerful, positive results? Let's consider another study, this time from medicine.

Dr. Nora Volkow, an expert on the brain and behavior, was part of an eight-year study on how to best treat students with ADHD. It is important to note that although there were medical interventions that yielded good results, this medical doctor gave a strong nod to the impact of what she termed *engaged teachers*. Here is an excerpt from an interview on the subject:

> Volkow, nonetheless, said she believes in trying behavioral therapies first, using drugs only if those aren't effective. She said her team's findings underscored the value of having teachers be as engaging as possible and of having parents reinforce good behavior with skillful praise and rewards.
>
> "Our brains are hard-wired to respond to bribes," she [Dr. Volkow] said.
>
> "And that goes even more so, apparently, for brains with ADHD." (Volkow, 2009)

This study is helpful to those of us who work in high-poverty sites and who wish to implement *Rich Brain, Poor Brain* strategies, for several reasons:

1. It underscores the power of engaged teachers who believe that their expectations and the decisions attached to them can change brains and behaviors.

2. Many of our students in high-poverty sites are diagnosed, whether correctly or inappropriately, with ADHD and other behavioral issues.

3. This may be because of the impacts of toxins in the environment or toxic expectations in the community.

4. Either way, teachers appear to be able to sway both biological and environmental threats against their students.

Moving forward into chapters 3-7, look for some of the ways that high expectations will be embedded in the *Rich Brain, Poor Brain* strategies.

Language

- Students can be expected to use words as currency.
- Teachers can be expected to demand rich, detailed language in the classroom.

Experiences

- Students can be expected to choose high-value coursework.
- Teachers can be expected to teach to the gifted in all classes.

Attitude

- Students can learn when they feel affirmed and capable.
- Teachers can train brains to be proactive, not reactive.

Performance

- Students can be expected to work hard.
- Teachers can shape performance through brain-friendly praise.

Let's pause to remember that many high-poverty or Title I sites are doing amazing work. I am writing this book to honor their work and to spread the word that an excellent education can be offered to all students when creativity and commitment to high expectations are set free. Still, there are places where change is needed.

Teachers who want to bring about change must believe first that they have the power within and without to do so. Our next Voice from the Field grew up in a rural area of the South and went on to become a recognized educator and school leader, both in the U.S. and in Ghana, West Africa. Let's hear what she has to say about empowering teachers, setting high expectations for children, and involving the community.

Voices from the Field:
Priscilla Johnson

Title I teacher, instructional coach in a Title I school, participant in a teaching program in Ghana, West Africa

"Just a little while ago, I had a conversation with my mom concerning my new position as an Instructional Technology Specialist and my future aspirations of becoming a school principal. I expressed how grateful I was for this opportunity to learn something new, to be challenged, and to gain perspective on how we all make this education thing work. The one thing I appreciate about my parents, and the village that has surrounded me my entire life, is that they literally believe I CAN DO ANYTHING. In any personal endeavors of which I have felt inadequate, insufficient, or unequipped to persevere through to completion, my village had already moved onto supporting my next aspiration. Why? Well, it's because they never doubted that I would achieve the first goal, so by moving on to the next goal, they are in turn celebrating the inevitable success that I will achieve, and reminding me of my end game at the same time. Without even saying it, they encourage me not to give up on my dreams, and they propel me subconsciously into believing that I'm unstoppable. Imagine if all children, regardless of whether they hail from an affluent or underprivileged background, had a village comprised of parents, teachers and community members who made them feel like they were unstoppable. It's really something to think about, isn't it?"

"Windsor Hill Arts Infused Elementary School is that place. I have seen first-hand as a 10-year educator in this Title I school how our village of stakeholders believes in every student's abilities and sets high expectations for learning. The result? Our students have risen to the occasion every time. As a recipient of the Kennedy Center for Performing Arts Distinction in Arts Education Award rated Excellent three years consecutively, our students have not only blown our minds academically and on state-mandated testing, but they are state and national title holders in contests including Doodle 4 Google and the annual National PTA Reflections Contest. They have been nurtured and challenged to celebrate their artistic gifts, and in turn have put their talents on display in extraordinary ways, such as having starring roles in weekly TV dramas and films, as well as showcasing visual art in venues that range from South Carolina to New York. In a school in which the percentage of students that qualify for free and reduced lunches exceeds 80%, these types of accomplishments are almost unheard of, but our village sets the stage for excellence each day. Mediocrity is not an option here. When teachers are empowered to dismiss the notion that where a student comes from determines their academic outcome, there is no glass ceiling high enough to close in the heights of which their students will reach."

Summary of Chapter Two's Big Ideas

- Expectations are powerful and shape our beliefs, decisions, and choices about students and schools.

- Expectations for students who live in poverty and those who come from more wealthy backgrounds are often different and drive outcomes in opposing directions.

- Expectations are difficult to maintain and nurture when teachers are working without support and in a constant state of stress.

- Teachers' expectations can change brains, but only when teachers believe that to be true and are given autonomy to operate as highly qualified professionals.

- Expecting change when one does the same thing over and over again is foolish. It is time to do a new thing in schools.

Chapter Three ● ● ● ● ● ● ●

LEAP Across the Gap with Language

We believe that the poverty of vocabulary should be discussed with the same passion as child hunger. —Too Small to Fail, The Clinton Foundation

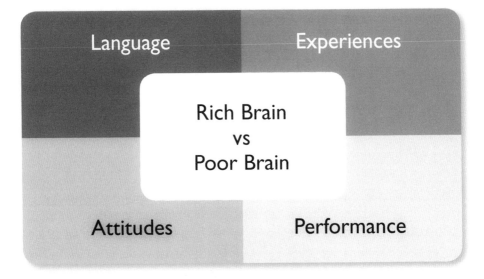

Language | Experiences

Rich Brain
vs
Poor Brain

Attitudes | Performance

Language, Language, Language

When selling a house, realtors are fond of the phrase "location, location, location." We have all heard that saying. What you might not know, realize, understand, or embrace in your heart and mind is the mantra for bridging social and synaptic gaps for all children: *language, language, language*.

Language in all four paradigms of listening, speaking, reading and writing is the real cognitive and social currency of our times. One of the greatest differences between rich-brain schools and poor-brain schools can be found in the myriad of ways that language is taught, brokered, used, abused, or shared. In this chapter, we will look at:

1. Differences between the ways in which rich-brain schools use language to thrive and poor-brain schools use language to survive

2. The language gap and why it is so dangerous

3. Three creative and inexpensive ways to bridge that gap

Rich Brain–Poor Brain Language Disparities

The following graphic shows what I perceive as the disparities that do damage to poor students. This interpretation is based on my review of the literature, my 30 years as an educator, and my work as a consultant to schools that range from very wealthy and successful to very poor and on the endangered species list. I have seen it all, and it all comes down to language—the organic and genuine currency for humans. Those who can use rich, varied, confident speech, who can read critically, who can write with clarity and creativity, and who can listen with active, inquisitive ears have a much greater chance for success in school and in life.

Disparities That Do Damage to Poor Students

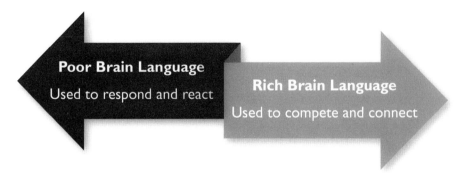

Poor Brain Language
Used to respond and react

Rich Brain Language
Used to compete and connect

Before moving to the chart on the next page, take a minute to note that the disparities that I share are based on what I have seen and what seems to be typical in sites that are not successful. A high-poverty site that has made great strides in creating a culture of literacy would not fit this template.

Poor-Brain Schools and Language	Rich-Brain Schools and Language
Children come to school with millions fewer words in their repertoire.	Children come to school speaking in complete sentences and often reading on their own already.
Children own fewer books of their own, and school libraries often lack large media centers because their locations are not attractive to media specialists who might have to travel long distances to the sites.	Children own many books of their own and have diverse, well-appointed school libraries. Their media centers are the heart of the school and serve as "mini colleges" with a mentor ready to help with research.
Families and school sites may not possess the items that create a culture of literacy, such as books, magazine subscriptions, electronic readers, or daily newspapers.	Families and school sites possess many items that create a culture of literacy, such as books, magazine subscriptions, electronic readers, and daily newspapers.
Parents typically have less formal education and may not enjoy reading.	Parents are typically well-educated, and their children see them reading or using language to build connections and to improve their status.
There are fewer opportunities for travel or enrichment that build *schema*, or language, about subjects. For example, going to the beach builds schema for the marine environment.	Travel is a natural extension of the curriculum. There are trips to the pumpkin patch in the fall, holiday music shows at winter break, and a spring break study trip. Rich-brain families and schools consider excursions to be part of the curriculum, not a luxury.
Adults may not have the time or luxury of interacting with children in social or personal ways that build expressive language. For example, a grandmother caring for several small children will be in survival mode, making sure the children are all safe and fed. She may not have time to discuss the weather or to read a story.	Adults provide a constant, interpersonal focus on building language. Children are read to, taken to libraries, or offered extracurricular opportunities that build schema. Rich-brain schools feature authors in residence, author studies, and book clubs.
Course syllabi in poor-brain sites often reflect a textbook-only curriculum. For example, in a gifted or honors class, there would not be a focus on reading multiple outside novels or sources.	Course syllabi in rich-brain sites include multiple literary sources, often done in thematic context. For example, in a unit on the Revolutionary War, students might read both *Johnny Tremain* and *Sarah Bishop* to get both male and female perspectives.

32

What Kinds of Language Experiences and Opportunities Do Poor Students Miss?

- Exposure to rich, detailed language from teachers trained as ELA masters
- A wide variety of literature across all subject areas
- Full integration of listening, speaking, reading, and writing
- Interfacing with authors, columnists and media experts who drift into the school world from their families and communities
- The ability to acquire a broad and deep cache of words during school because they come to school prepared to be readers

Revisiting the Language Gap

- According to the Hart and Ridley studies, there is a 30-million-word gap between rich and poor children by the age of 3. (Hart & Ridley, 2003)
- While half of middle-income children in 4th grade are considered proficient, closer to 17% of low-income 4th graders earn proficient marks. (Annie E. Casey Foundation, 2010)
- Early reading skills predict general academic performance, and early deficits reduce the likelihood of catching up later on. (Whitehurst, 1998)
- 70% of poor children live in single-parent families, while only 6% of affluent children live in single-parent homes, a statistic that often means fewer opportunities for reading, language, and building word currency.

What Evidence Do We Have to Make This Point?

When I visit rich-brain sites, whether public or private, I see and hear what I call the "Luxury of Language":

- Books everywhere and across all subject areas
- Students reading for pleasure and for research
- Displays on authors and reading initiatives
- Evidence of drama, writing, and debate
- Journals for all subject areas
- Anchor charts that demonstrate a commitment to using detailed, evidence-based responses

I do not typically see these things in poor-brain sites. Not often. Not usually. So what can be done?

Clearly these are huge and complex issues, and it is not the intent of this small book to solve them. However, it is my intention to replicate experiences that rich brains rely on to build language with inexpensive knockoffs, such as the three strategies that follow.

Strategy One: School Read-Aloud Model

Rationale

Students come to school with fewer words and with fewer opportunities to make up that word gap. Reading aloud daily and targeting high-value language that is tied to high-stakes assessments is a free and powerful way to bridge social and synaptic gaps. This model is designed for maximum language growth with minimal financial output. Moreover, it is seamless, designed to embed into the daily schedule with only a 10-minute commitment that is tied to science and social studies vocabulary and schema. Reading aloud is free, fun, fair, accessible, and available.

Purpose of the Initiative

- To increase students' vocabulary and fluency through an embedded read-aloud model
- Use classical and vetted children's literature tied to high-stakes science and social studies standards
- Focus on reading so that students can hear and absorb more words

Why does it work so well?

- Chunking standards and themes with language builds vocabulary and fluency.
- Framing literacy levels the playing field, taps the affective domain, and encourages visualization.
- By the time a student leaves elementary school, he or she would have experienced many of the best pieces of children's literature which are tied to important standards. Students therefore build schema and vocabulary for some of the toughest to teach concepts and ideas.

How do we make it happen?

Using the template on the following pages, create a schoolwide literacy model to match your school's interests, the curriculum, and teachers' styles. I have included a list of resources to help select books, as well as a sample matrix that has been used successfully in multiple sites. This works when it is consistently done every day, in every grade, and using specific books tied to high-value vocabulary.

Voices from the Field:
Johnnie Boatwright
Title I Leader, South Carolina

"I have spent 30 years in the field, most of them in Title I settings, and few things have been as exciting to implement as the Read-Aloud Model. It is organic, simple, realistic, and it works. We have seen teachers become excited about the joys of literature and students want to read more and more often. Although the model is tied to current brain research, which is important to me as a leader, I am most satisfied with the simplicity and joy that we bring to classrooms with 10 minutes of reading aloud daily from high quality children's literature."

Grade	1st Quarter	2nd Quarter	3rd Quarter	4th Quarter
2	Book: Key Concept(s):	Book: Key Concept(s):	Book: Key Concept(s):	Book: Key Concept(s):
3	Book: Key Concept(s):	Book: Key Concept(s):	Book: Key Concept(s):	Book: Key Concept(s):
4	Book: Key Concept(s):	Book: Key Concept(s):	Book: Key Concept(s):	Book: Key Concept(s):
5	Book: Key Concept(s):	Book: Key Concept(s):	Book: Key Concept(s):	Book: Key Concept(s):

Remember, this model works because the books you choose have key concepts for high-value vocabulary targets in science and social studies embedded in the stories. You are sneaking them in with a story, much like a savvy parent blends an egg into the milkshake of a sickly toddler. The list below contains some vetted sources for setting up your own site's matrix.

Reading Lists for Brian Framing

- IRA Children's Book Award – www.reading.org
- Notable Children's Book Awards – www.ncte.org
- Young Reader's Choice – www.pnla.org/yrca/index.htm
- Parent's Choice Awards – www.parents-choice.org/allawards.cfm
- The Newbery and Caldecott Medals – www.ala.org
- The Coretta Scott King Award – www.ala.org
- Book Sense Book of the Year Award – www.bookweb.org/btw/awards
- The Jefferson Cup – www.fairfaxcounty.gov/library/reading/ya/jeffcup.htm

Sample Matrix for Grades 2-5

Grade	1st Quarter	2nd Quarter	3rd Quarter	4th Quarter	Notes
2	**Communities** *Because of Winn Dixie* Kate DiCamillo	**Culture Differences** *Extra Credit* Andrew Clements (Girl) (Boy)	**Matter & Inquiry** *Charlie and the Chocolate Factory* Roald Dahl	**Habitats - Problem Solving** *Charlotte's Web* E. B. White	• curiosity • attitudes • compassion • multiple perspectives
3	**Time and Place SC Settings** *Stranded* Idella Bodie (Boy)	**Revolutionary War** *The Swamp Fox of the Revolution* Stewart H. Holbrook (Boy)	**Animals -Environments, Habitats** *Rabbit Hill* Robert Lawson	**Civil Rights** *The Watsons Go to Birmingham* Christopher Paul Curtis (Boy)	• heritage • adversity • inquiry • conflict
4	**Native Americans** *Walk Two Moons* Sharon Creech (Girl)	*Where the Mountain Meets the Moon* Grace Lin	**Revolutionary War** *The Fighting Ground* Edward Irving Wortis	**Westward Expansion, Explorers** *Caddie Woodlawn* Carol Ryrie Brink	• perseverance • challenge • stereotypes • family structure • gender roles • arts imagination • multiple intelligences
5	**Great Depression** *Esperanza Rising* Pam Munoz Ryan (Girl)	**Ocean and Landforms** *Island of the Blue Dolphins* Scott O'Dell (Girl)	**Holocaust** *The Boy in Striped Pajamas* John Boyne	**Physics** *A Wrinkle in Time* Madeleine L'Engle	• community • dynamics • roles • diversity • friendship • transitions • character building • characterization

Strategy Two: The Rise of the Greek and Roman Literacy Empires and More

A second strategy, or actually a patchwork of strategies, that can be effective is designed to take the language that children already bring to school and multiply it exponentially. We take what they know and go with it. There is much attention paid to the language gap, and it is warranted. But what if we switch things around in our minds, and, instead of lamenting what our students don't have in their language stores, take those words and do a "loaves and fishes" (pardon the Biblical pun) thing?

There are two common practices I see in rich-brain sites that could be replicated with relative ease in any site and deliver maximum results in terms of language development:

1. The use of anchor charts to maintain a constant, vigilant attention to the proper use of language, especially in the question-response mode.

2. The implementation of a Greek and Latin stem program to exponentially increase both receptive and expressive language.

Receptive language emerges first. These are the words that students hear, understand, and can act upon in listening and reading.

Expressive language emerges from receptive language. These are the words that students can actively use in speaking and writing.

Rationale

Students come to school with fewer words and with fewer opportunities to make up that word gap. Implementing both anchor charts for the desired use of language and a Greek and Latin stem program to increase vocabulary can help to LEAP social and synaptic gaps, especially the word gap. Like the Reading Aloud model, this piece is designed for maximum language growth with minimal financial output. It is also embedded into the daily schedule with a small time commitment that is tied to listening, speaking, reading, and writing standards.

Anchors Away

One of the simplest strategies to capture rich language that teachers want students to use is the ubiquitous *anchor chart*. Too rudimentary? Think again. The right anchor charts placed everywhere and used every day become currency. Students have access to what they need and to what teachers expect right in front of them. They are never put on the spot. They just turn to the right place to use the words they have and attach them to the words they need. If we do this enough, neural pathways become hard-wired.

There are numerous benefits to using anchor charts to create a rich-brain classroom:

- Anchor charts are ideal for replicating key language interactions that many students miss out on in their early years.
- Anchor charts keep teachers focused on language goals.
- Anchor charts encourage a constructivist style of teaching and learning.
- Anchor charts are inexpensive.
- Anchor charts are a tool for both students and teachers.

Surprisingly, in many sites, especially the most language-barren sites, I do not see anchor charts for ELA. But in sites that are already language-rich, they are a staple!

There are at least four types of anchor charts that we need to do the heavy lifting of replicating rich-brain language:

1. Inference
2. Critical thinking
3. Complete sentences
4. Greek and Latin stems (detailed in the next section)

Pinterest has a treasure trove of anchor chart examples – I encourage you to check them out. Simply navigate to www.pinterest.com, search the phrase *anchor chart* and go to town!

Greek and Roman Stem Vocabulary

There are many inexpensive commercial Greek and Roman stem vocabulary builders. There are workbooks, electronic whiteboard lessons, online computer programs, or teachers can simply build their own. The following pages include slides from a workshop that I do with high-poverty students. If I were teaching this, I would do a "Stem-a-Day to Keep the Doctor Away" kind of thing and put this up with the bell work or as an anticipatory set for daily ELA.

Importance

- Knowing and using Greek and Latin word roots can help you figure out the meaning of words you don't recognize.

Why is it important to know how to use Greek and Latin word roots?

P/S; CFU x1-2

- This will make you a better reader and writer.

Can anyone share a different reason?

Volunteers

We know that words are broken into parts that help us figure out their meaning:

Prefixes:
- *un-*   **undo**
- *re-*   **refill**
- *pro-*   **for, forward**

Prefixes are at the beginning of words.

  pre- means before
  fix *means attach, repair*

Suffixes:
- *-ful*   **joyful**
- *-ly*   **sadly**
- **-ness** **kindness**

Suffixes are at the end of words.

So, "prefix" means "attached before."

Whiteboards: *Which word part is found at the end of words?*

APK

Here's an example using a state standard, showing how nicely this kind of addition can mix into the curriculum:

5th Grade ELA Standard
Word Analysis & Vocabulary 1.4

Know abstract, derived roots and affixes from Greek and Latin and use this knowledge to analyze the meaning of complex words.

Skill Steps

1. Highlight the word root (or roots).
   - What does the word root mean?
2. Look at the remainder of the word:
   - What does the prefix mean?
   - What does the suffix mean?
3. Use the word root table to determine the meaning.

Skill

Perhaps you are thinking, "We already cover this in ELA." Perhaps you do, maybe once a year, and then check off a specific standard. What I am proposing is a daily dose of Greek and Latin in the Title I classroom. Look at it this way: affluent students have doctors, lawyers, professors, engineers and architects sitting at the dinner table with them or helping them with their homework. These professionals use language that relies on a visceral knowledge of Greek and Latin stems to make a living. They transfer this knowledge to their offspring and friends in conversation and other contractual agreements. We must replicate this language on a daily basis by layering Greek and Latin stems into our conversations and contractual agreements in the classroom. I am including a link to one model that I have actually used with children that has collected good data on its success:

> **It's All Greek to Me!**
>
> Look at it this way: affluent students have doctors, lawyers, professors, engineers and architects sitting at the dinner table with them or helping them with their homework. These professionals use language that relies on a visceral knowledge of Greek and Latin stems to make a living.

http://eps.schoolspecialty.com/products/literacy/vocabulary/wordly-wise-3000-3rd-edition

I have no affiliation with this group, but I have seen enough to recommend it. It is called *Wordly Wise*. The group has been around for a long time and offers paper-and-pencil as well as online versions. In addition, and something that I find very interesting given our first strategy, they utilize a read-aloud model to increase science and social studies vocabulary.

There are also a number of commercial products that seem up to the job. Here are two examples; a workbook model, as well as a stem chart from which teachers would create their own daily exercises.

1. *Greek and Latin Roots*, by Trisha Callella, Creative Teaching Press, 2004
2. *Language Die-Cut Magnets, Greek/Latin Roots*, Ashley Productions Inc.

Another vetted source will be cited at the end of this chapter by our "Voice from the Field," Professor Rick Blanchard.

Strategy Three: Book Clubs, Reading Initiatives, and Celebrity Readers

Rationale

Like our previous two strategies, implementing book clubs, reading initiatives, and celebrity readers to increase reading for pleasure and purpose can help to LEAP social and synaptic gaps, especially the word gap. This piece is also designed for maximum language growth with minimal financial output. Moreover, these strategies are designed to be integrated into the school day either during assembly times, homeroom meetings, or most beautifully, in the extended-day enrichment piece.

How Do We Do It?

In affluent sites, books and authors are not foreign or far away. They are acknowledged as friends and family. Becoming a writer oneself, or having an author at dinner, or hearing a parent read aloud from a newspaper op-ed piece written by a neighbor are natural, normal experiences. These are not typical experiences in high-poverty schools and homes, so we must embed replications of these experiences in what I call a *Celebrate Literacy* piece.

Celebrate Literacy	
Participate in national literacy celebrations such as Read for the Record.	Invite celebrity readers in to coordinate with national events, such as U.S. Constitution Day.

Through local, state, and national initiatives	
Establish book clubs that provide snacks and copies of the books.	Participate in state events, such as voting on favorite new juvenile novels.

And through daily literacy connections beyond the lesson plan	
Investigate grants for "authors in residence" through local arts councils.	Publish student writing, and post it consistently and conspicuously.

One of my favorite projects, and one in which I have involved my future teachers, is *Read for the Record*. You can find more information at www.jstart.org. Each year, a children's book is selected to be read aloud at thousands of schools around the nation on the same day. The book is provided online that day, via a downloadable link, so it doesn't cost a dime! Creating a schoolwide celebration with celebrity readers (such as local dignitaries, high school or college coaches, the PTA president, or the city fire chief) invited to attend can be motivating and memorable.

Celebrate Literacy is designed to do three things: 1) infiltrate the school and home with a luxurious level of vocabulary and ideas; 2) infuse a sense of urgency and excitement about listening, speaking, reading, and writing; and 3) insist that all children have the option to own, touch, experience, and enjoy as many forms of literacy as possible, no matter their income level or parents' educational status.

To that end, sites that want to become "literacy celebrators" should check off as many items as they can on the following list:

Idea or Event	Does It Cost Dollars or Sense? ("sense" meaning *free* and *creative*)	Are you doing or can you do it?
Create book clubs for both boys and girls to capture gender-based interests.	Both $ and Sense • Use mini grants from PTA • Ask organizations like the Junior Service League to donate the books.	
Volunteer to be a site to choose your state's children's book award winner each year, and feed those titles into the book clubs mentioned above.	Sense Only • Connect with your state library association	
Establish classroom reading areas with lots of leveled books, but also stuffed animals to cuddle, puppets to tell the story, and comfortable sitting spots.	Sense Only • Gather books from the public library discard pile, yard sales, retired teachers • Use Facebook or other social media to ask retired teachers to give you their books	

Idea or Event	Does It Cost Dollars or Sense? ("sense" meaning *free* and *creative*)	Are you doing or can you do it?
Send books home. To keep. Yes, to keep. Remember, affluent students own as many as 100 books of their OWN by age 10. We are trying to replicate that feeling of being a reader, and not just at school! I love the model in which children first take a book home and do something with it, such as read to a sibling or parent and then keep it forever.	Both $ and Sense • Leftover fund from your annual budget • PTA fund-raiser • Mini grants from local businesses • Additional grant suggestions: Diversity in Action (http://dia.ala.org/content/alsc-awards-mini-grants-15-libraries-start-d%C3%ADa-family-book-clubs); The Ezra Jack Keats Foundation (http://www.ezra-jack-keats.org/section/ezra-jack-keats-mini-grant-program-for-public-libraries-public-schools/); The Meemic Foundation (https://www.meemic.com/the-meemic-foundation.aspx); Students Need to Read (http://www.studentsneedtoread.org/)	
Coordinate a "Celebrate Literacy" event each fall to kick off the school year. Introduce your Read-Aloud model with a large, laminated poster of the matrix and sample of the books.	Sense Only • Connect this to the Read-Aloud model and get a layered effect	
Use celebrity readers at least once per quarter. How? At the "Celebrate Literacy" kick-off, at the PTA meeting, or during a school festival as a "booth" where students can hear the fire chief or the local minister reading aloud from favorite books.	Sense Only • Build a culture of community excitement about books	

46

Voices from the Field:
Dana Clerico Hedgepeth, M.Ed.

*Teacher of the Year, National Board Certified in social studies,
and former English-language teacher in China*

"We are all English-language learners in America, all through our lives. This hit home for my husband and I as we taught English in China for three years. We taught kindergarten through adults, public and private, students who were fluent and wanted to learn more together with students who could barely say, 'I'm fine thanks, and you?' It was challenging, stressful, and often a unique juggling act, and one of the greatest experiences I have had in my life. If you're familiar with the children's story *The Little Old Man Who Could Not Read* by Irma Simonton Black and Seymour Fleishman, that's how I felt in so many circumstances during our first year. I walked aimlessly around supermarkets looking for something familiar, purchased a pot of espresso instead of regular coffee one Sunday simply because it was the cheaper price. Life is hard, embarrassing, and intimidating when you are unable to read."

"Everyone is an English-language learner. As a middle school social studies teacher, my classes are heterogeneously mixed and differentiation is a must, and so my test items are written to cover content and yet match the frustrating reading levels of a mixed group of readers. I am always teaching reading, even when I am teaching social studies."

"So, reinforcing reading and vocabulary skills throughout everyday lessons is a critical component of my classes. Reading through a document together, I tell my students, 'Ok guys, get out your pens, pencils, or highlighters, and here we go.' As I read aloud, I draw their attention to Greek or Latin stems in a word. For example, in a lesson on the Scientific Revolution, my students underlined *g e o* in the word geocentric and wrote *earth* over the three letters. We then did the same for *h e l i o* in heliocentric, *a s t r o* in astronomer, and *t h e o* in theocracy. Students responded well to this strategy, and one student told me the following week that there was a word that he was able to figure out on a benchmark, web-based language arts assessment because of one these mini-lessons in my room. Helping students break words down into smaller parts gives them more confidence when approaching a word they do not know and greater tenacity to try their best to determine its meaning. Strategies that expand language fluency and flexibility are critical for all of us, because we are all English-language learners."

Voices from the Field:
Rick Blanchard

Professor of Education and former state-level director of gifted education

"Putting on my 'gifted and talented' hat, I firmly believe that gifted and talented students are found in all economic groups and are often under-represented in high-poverty sites. For gifted or potentially gifted students (not yet identified), overcoming a vocabulary deficit is paramount. Word etymology is one powerful way for students to make up some ground with vocabulary development. One series I have used with surity is *Word Within the Word* by Michael Clay Thompson."

"One of the most intriguing works is Michael Clay Thompon's ten year study of classic literature, in which he studied 130 works and compiled the 100 most frequently used vocabulary words from these works. The list is a free download at http://www.rfwp.com/book/classic-words."

"Immersion in good literature is essential for high-poverty students to bridge synaptic gaps. Another colleague, Tamra Stambaugh and her mentor, Joyce Van Tassel-Baska, developed a series entitled *Jacob's Ladder* which helps to bridge gaps in reading comprehension. After some targeted research that found students of poverty needing some scaffolding and modeling to grasp higher-level concepts, they worked to develop the Jacob's Ladder series, full of great 'ladders' to help scaffold students quickly to reach reading comprehension heights by using high-interest reading selections. When working with potentially gifted students, especially those who come from high-poverty backgrounds, meet each student where she or he is and take her or him to new heights."

Summary of Chapter Three's Big Ideas

- Words are currency and power. By giving children more and better words, we give them the means to change their lives.

- Building a culture of literacy at school can diffuse some of the damage that occurs when there is not a culture of literacy at home.

- Reading aloud in a targeted, daily program is an inexpensive and powerful way to build word currency across high-value language targets.

- Using strategies such as anchor charts and teaching Greek and Latin stems can bridge the language gap by giving students models and material to increase their own word power.

- Establishing book clubs, bringing in celebrity readers, and participating in national initiatives for reading sends a message that literacy is valuable and enjoyable, and also helps to replicate the cultural and familiar language experiences that affluent students often enjoy at home.

Chapter Four ● ● ● ● ● ● ●

LEAP Across the Gap with Experiences

When you challenge other people's ideas of who or how you should be, they may try to diminish and disgrace you. It can happen in small ways in hidden places, or in big ways on a world stage. You can spend a lifetime resenting the tests, angry about the slights and the injustices. Or, you can rise above it.

— Carly Fiorina

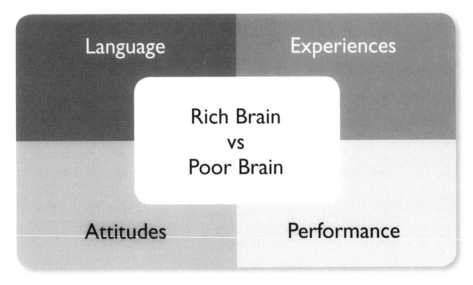

Language   Experiences

Rich Brain
vs
Poor Brain

Attitudes   Performance

Whether you call it experiential learning, social learning theory or constructivism, students who come from more affluent homes and who, by design and good fortune, attend more affluent schools, have advantages that their less-wealthy peers do not enjoy. That is a very nice and politically correct way of saying there are "haves and have nots" (which my mother always said) in the world. Truth be told, this has always been the case. Remember the whole feudal system chart that most of us had to replicate in 9th grade world history?

We like to believe that we have moved on, evolved, done better, and in many ways we have. Indeed, many high-poverty sites in urban, suburban, and rural settings have made great strides in serving the needs of all students. Still, in our country, as in many parts of the world, there are "haves and have nots" in public schools. Remember my original plan – to provide quality, classy "knock-off" experiences that replicate the fancier, more expensive experiences that wealthy schools provide? In this chapter, we will examine three ways to provide *experiences*, the E in the LEAP model.

Whether you call it experiential learning, social learning theory or constructivism, students who come from more affluent homes and who, by design and good fortune, attend more affluent schools, have advantages that their less wealthy peers do not enjoy.

Specifically, this chapter offers three specific strategies to shape the experiences in high-poverty or even more ordinary sites:

Advanced Coursework: AP, Not IEP

Think Globally

Interns Wanted

Connect to the Real World

To replicate the experiences that brains impacted by poverty need to compete academically and socially, schools need to think in terms of advanced coursework, global experiences, and real-world career proficiencies. Cost is always a factor, but making adjustments to course syllabi, using technology more effectively and collaborating with partners to the fullest extent can do a great deal to LEAP across social and synaptic gaps.

Strategy One: AP, Not IEP

The most essential idea in this section is the commitment to more honors and AP courses at every opportunity, whether students qualify using the traditional assessments or not. I believe we have to have a "build it and they will come" mentality with rigorous coursework, and that this must begin as early as possible.

Rationale

When I visit classrooms, speak at conferences or interact with teachers, the consensus is that a great deal of attention is paid to things like RTI and low-performing students. Our focus is on weaknesses and testing, testing, testing. Do we really believe that identifying weaknesses among students is going to tell us anything new? We know these students have issues. What if we stopped the constant testing and just assume that yes, students have weak areas in their cognitive domains and just proceed with plans to immerse all students in an enriched and challenging curriculum to see what happens?

Schools offering AP exams to one or more students, by year

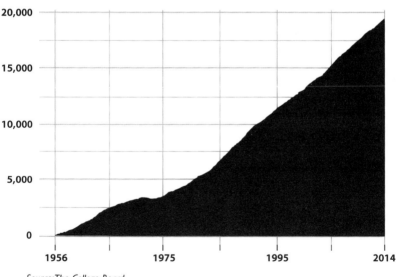

Source: The College Board

As the graph above suggests, there has been an impressive increase in AP course offerings, but not all students have been invited to the AP dance. When we look at the offerings by region, the poorest areas of our country have fewer AP classes.

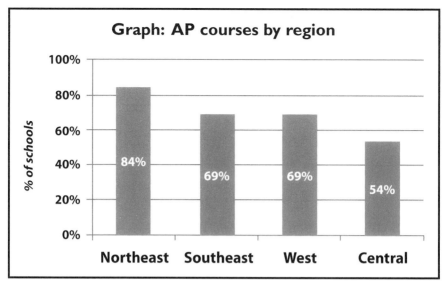

Graph: AP courses by region

Source: The College Board

Yet it appears that when students do take AP courses, whether they pass or not, there is a positive outcome. Being a part of a rigorous school experience changes students' performance and personal beliefs about what is possible.

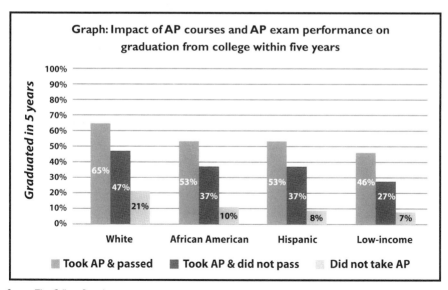

Graph: Impact of AP courses and AP exam performance on graduation from college within five years

Source: The College Board

Is High School Enough?

In the pivotal report *Is High School Enough?* (Center for Public Education, 2012), inequities in high school experiences are examined. These disparities can be extrapolated to understand the three big ideas offered in this chapter.

> Research shows that students who take rigorous courses in high school are more likely to get into, and succeed, in college. For a lot of students though, especially low-income and minority students, AP courses haven't always been an option. North County Principal Julie Cares says five years ago, only 10 percent of the school's 2,000 students took any Advanced Placement classes. Less than one-fourth of seniors planned to attend a four-year college.

> "When I first came, there was a sense of, just low expectations," she says. "A lot of students not only didn't believe it was possible, but it didn't even occur to them that was something they might do." (Scott, 2015)

How Do We Do It?

I propose five strategies to increase rigor in course offerings. These are not new, but I can tell you from my work in schools around the country that they are not happening in many places where they are most needed.

I was invited to review course syllabi for an honors ELA course in a high-poverty site that was under scrutiny by the state. The course syllabus listed only a textbook – no outside novels at all for a middle school honors course. In a more affluent school, just 10 miles away, the same course syllabus contained eight outside novels, focusing on two each quarter. You might be thinking, "Well, the parents cannot afford the outside books, so teachers did not add them to the syllabus." That might be the case, except for the fact that in a closet in the media center of the high-poverty site, gathering dust, sat class sets of hardcover, annotated novels by 25 different writers. Everyone in the school knew about the books as well as the Title I dollars used to purchase them, but they had never been checked out. I talked with the ELA teachers, who seemed uncomfortable with the whole idea of using the novels. The department chair finally admitted, "Dr. B, I have not read most of those books myself, so I would be one chapter ahead of the students. I am not going to be embarrassed in that way."

Rigor. We talk about it, but our fears and our own beliefs about what is possible for all students can get in the way of change. We need change if we want to embody the belief system that proclaims "AP, not IEP!" Remember chapter two? Students whose teachers have high expectations will rise up to meet those expectations.

Let's look at five strategies for raising rigor:

 1. Add outside reading to all ELA courses grades 5 and above. Use grants and Title I funds for materials.

 2. Expand honors courses to include more students.

 3. Increase AP offerings by using virtual school technology.

 4. Create peer study groups for honors and AP classes so that students receive support.

 5. Require all teachers to do long-range plans (grades 1-5) and course syllabi (grades 6-12). Have a "Rigor Report" team that examines them to insure that challenging experiences occur.

Prepare the Community for this Change

In my work on task forces and program evaluations concerning AP and honors course implementation in high-poverty sites, two issues emerge:

1. Students who qualify do not want to take the more rigorous courses.

2. Parents do not push their children to take the advanced courses.

There is, in many communities, schools and families, a stigma associated with these rigorous courses. We need to talk about these issues openly and provide a safe place for students to choose AP and honors, even when their peers make other choices and their families question the decision to take advanced courses. In my own family, there was tacit pressure to "stay in my place." I understood that writing a paper for an honors class or conjugating French verbs came after I had done my chores, cooked a meal for the family while my mother was at work, or taken care of my baby brother.

> "AP, not IEP" is about more than courses. Therefore, I suggest that sites that want to bring about change need to commit sizeable resources to supporting students who choose rigorous courses, not just to the courses themselves.

One of the key ideas in this book is the understanding that more affluent or rich-brain students do not question the choice of AP or honors; it is the natural course of things. For students in high-poverty sites, these rigorous courses mean taking a different path, perhaps one that nobody else in the family has taken. There may be little support and even discouragement. Therefore, I suggest that sites that want to bring about change commit sizeable resources to supporting students who choose rigorous courses, not just to the courses themselves. Simply providing AP or honors courses is not enough. Students and families need to be introduced to and supported through what may be a new academic paradigm.

What might this support look like? I have seen a number of viable options in sites around the country:

- Counselors and teachers trained to mentor students through AP and honors
- Teaching students the soft skills required for internal locus of control, delaying gratification, study time, and advanced planning
- Creating learning communities for these students, with study groups, snacks, peer tutors, and even shirts and backpacks
- Pairing high school AP students with middle school honors students for luncheons, book talks, and field trips
- Trying a flipped classroom model where students have more time to engage with teachers instead of reading
- Designing courses that block subjects, such as social studies and ELA, so that students can "double dip" and get more mileage out of reading and projects

In closing this section, I will share a personal story that provokes me to remain committed to helping teachers look beyond what they think they see in a child who comes from a less-than-affluent home. I was in the third grade when we moved to the rural south. Previously, I had been educated in high-quality DOD schools as my father was in the military. In those schools, I was identified as gifted since I read at the high-school level by second grade. When my dad was transferred to South Carolina, we moved off base to a small town where social class was hard-wired into every decision. The school principal at my new school made a quick judgement when she saw my family and assigned me to the remedial reading group. I was horrified. These students were working in a phonics workbook, and most could not even read. I tried to tell the teacher that there was a mistake, but she brushed me off. Fortunately I saw a small group of students leave to go to a "special class," and they carried with them the same green book that I had used in my gifted reading class in New York. I went up to the teacher and told her that I was supposed to be in that group. She asked, and I will never forget this, "Are you sure you can read that book?" I took her own teacher's copy of the book from her desk and began to read aloud from the teacher's directions for the lesson. She looked horrified and summoned the principal. They both stared at me as if I had horns, and then dispatched me down the hall to the gifted reading group. I remember feeling two things very clearly: 1) something bad would happen to me if I had to stay in the lower reading group; and 2) these people did not like me and did not know me, and I was insulted. Most eight-year-olds do not have that kind of audacity, cheek, chutzpah, or whatever you want to call it. I believe it was divine intervention, a force pushing me forward to be able to write this book and help other children who are judged by their family's income, not their intellect.

Strategy Two: Think Globally

In our quest to level the playing field, to embed equitable experiences, to enrich neural pathways before pruning can set in and damage potential, we must consider innovative ways to involve our less wealthy, typically more isolated students. We might pursue this exposure and enrichment in two ways: 1) taking the students out into the world whenever possible; and 2) bringing the world to the students, which is often more doable. Let's talk about both.

Field trips are expensive, right? Not always. With sponsors and taking advantage of special discounts and deals, trips to local art, nature and historical sites need not be prohibitive. The best strategy is good planning. Start by setting a goal of one field trip per semester.

Rationale

Thinking globally is about more than just exposure and enrichment. It is about diffusing the threat of nihilism that so often pervades the lives of students who fight to make it in tough economic and social circumstances. They often feel that nothing matters other than the struggles in their daily paths.

How Do We Make It Happen?

Use the diagram below to break down the one-field-trip-per-semester goal into digestible parts.

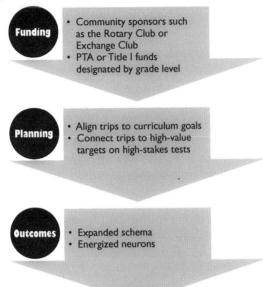

Funding
- Community sponsors such as the Rotary Club or Exchange Club
- PTA or Title I funds designated by grade level

Planning
- Align trips to curriculum goals
- Connect trips to high-value targets on high-stakes tests

Outcomes
- Expanded schema
- Energized neurons

Field trips, whether traditional or virtual, matter for six reasons. We will take the word GLOBAL and break it down to understand the importance of making the effort to include travel in the curriculum.

Gets students out into new places and among different people that increase interest in staying in school.

Lets students become a part of interesting, unusual experiences, sights, sounds and people that are not routinely found in their sphere of influence.

Opens students' ears to "the language of place" that expands their vocabularies. For example, at an aquarium, the language reflects the place and animals native there.

Balances the scales of experience among students. Everyone hears the same messages at the same time.

Allows students to practice desirable social behaviors in authentic settings.

Leads students to consider career paths in real time. It is one thing to talk about becoming a forest ranger; it is another to watch him or her at work while visiting a local wildlife refuge.

LEAP Across the Gap with Experiences | 90/1135LE

Going global does not always mean going out. For many reasons, not exclusively issues of dollars and distance, virtual trips abroad make sense in today's sites. Consider two additional "trips" each semester in virtual form. How can this be done? Let's take a quick trip to one of the most accessible and helpful sites I found while doing research for this chapter: Global Digital Citizen (http://globaldigitalcitizen.org/ten-of-the-best-virtual-field-trips).

> The benefits of virtual field trips are well known: They're inexpensive—often free—and are less time-consuming than a real trip. But researching which virtual field trips are best can prove labor-intensive, and many resources are out-of-date. To help educators save time, we've chosen these 10 virtual field trips based on their relevancy, depth and quality of resources, and potential for student excitement.
>
> – Global Digital Citizen

What kinds of virtual trips are found? Here's a sample of the offerings available through Global Digital Citizen:

- Arctic Adventure
- Hershey's Factory
- Le Louvre
- Mount Everest
- Museum of Natural History
- Seven Wonders of the World
- White House

Other sites such as the Sierra Club, the Smithsonian, the United States Holocaust Memorial Museum, dozens of impressive art galleries, the White House, as well as many government agencies feature interactive tours and lesson plans to go along with them. Students will feel connected to possibilities far beyond their ordinary world. As Pat Conroy said in his evocative novel about teaching on an island virtually cut off from the world, "The teacher must always be on the attack, looking for new ideas, changing worn-out tactics, and never, ever falling into patterns that lead to student ennui."

Links to Virtual Tours Worth Taking!

- http://teaching.monster.com/education/articles/
  8847-5-best-virtual-field-trips
  Rates the top five, including the Smithsonian

- http://www.virtualfreesites.com/us.government.html
  This is the mother lode! All of the agencies plus national treasures, and primary source docs to follow up with.

- http://www.educationworld.com/a_tech/tech/tech071.shtml
  Nice international selection

- http://www.ala.org/offices/resources/virtualfield
  The American Library Association's site, rich with art and humanities choices

- http://www.nationalww2museum.org/learn/education/for-teachers/
  distance-learning/virtual-field-trips.html
  National WWII Museum

- http://www.eschoolnews.com/2013/04/07/ten-of-the-best-virtual-field-trips/
  Takes you from Colonial Williamsburg to the Lascaux cave paintings

- http://www.discoveryeducation.com/northamerica/event.cfm
  Strong science and social studies content

- http://www.theteachersguide.com/virtualtours.html
  I love this one, sorted by grade levels

Strategy Three: Connect to the Real World

Like the global strategy in this chapter, the deliberate and determined plan to connect all students to real-world experiences that set them up to be successful in the workplace puts less-affluent students in situations that may be unfamiliar and yet essential.

To do this, I recommend three strategies that are either free or can be arranged with a modest budget. Each replicates experiences that wealthy, driven sites routinely do in order to make their graduates competitive in the workplace:

1. School uniforms

2. Current events as part of the curriculum

3. Career planning as a curriculum standard, not as a single day in the school year

LEAP *Across the Gap with Experiences* | 90/1135LE

Rationale

Wiring neural pathways for career success begins early and requires a specific set of experiences.

School Uniforms

I know it is a prickly topic, but I would be remiss by not listing it as a preferred strategy in the context of this book. Remember, we are attempting to replicate the experiences that rich-brain students have in their schools, and wearing uniforms is de rigueur. There is solid evidence that uniforms bring, well, uniformity to the school experience that can be valuable. Put it this way – putting on a uniform daily sends a message.

> **School is my business. School is my job.**

> **I wear a uniform when I go to work. My work is learning and thinking.**

> **My peers are wearing the uniform, too. We are all working toward the same goals in our business.**

Not long ago, I was visiting a school on the island of Barbados and talking with the school's principal. She asked me if it was true that students in the U.S. wear whatever they want to school. I told her that it was so. She frowned with what appeared to be disapproval and said, "So, your children are allowed to do whatever they want? To disrespect school by not wearing the school uniform? No wonder you have so many problems."

It was interesting to hear another voice. But what does the research tell us? There are relatively few studies, and the purpose of this chapter is not to do a review of the literature on uniforms. I do hear some common themes:

1. School uniforms may increase attendance rates.
2. Better attendance affects test scores and achievement.
3. Better achievement builds self-confidence and satisfaction with school.
4. Feeling more confident and part of a team increases positive behaviors and may reduce negative behaviors.

School uniforms set a tone of seriousness and professionalism that, I believe, shape neurons to create a schema for school behavior.

There are two concerns that arise concerning the question of school uniforms: cost and creativity. Let's consider both. Everyone has an opinion about school uniforms, and these opinions range widely. I spent some time talking with principals of Title I sites that do require uniforms, and they are pleased. Here are three takeaways from these school leaders:

- School uniforms are less expensive than regular clothes, especially when one chooses something simple like khaki pants and a navy polo shirt.

- Local churches, non-profits, and service groups often provide funds for the uniforms or the uniforms themselves.

- Uniforms seem helpful in reducing bullying and gang behaviors.

Finally, looking the part of a scholar is not a drain on creativity. It is a strategy to free the mind, allowing students to ignore teasing about what they wear or about who is more attractively dressed and to focus on learning.

Staying Current and Connected Builds Neuro-Connectivity

I will never forget a clinical teaching debacle in which I played the role of the fool. I was wrapping up my M.Ed. at a university lab school that catered to the children of the faculty. There were more BMWs in that school pickup line than I had ever seen in one place! I was doing an art activity with six-year-olds while being observed by a faculty member from behind the two-way mirror. The lesson was going nicely until a very erudite child corrected me on my geography. He and his family had gone away for a long weekend to Florence to visit his grandmother, and he was sharing about the trip. Now in my part of the South, Florence is a mid-sized town known for pecan groves and barbeque. "Did you eat at the Barbeque Barn? " I inquired. The child looked dubious, then laughed. "Of course not," he said. "I meant Florence, Italy, and we had pasta." My university supervisor was critical of my lack of sophistication. I should have realized, she pointed out, who I was dealing with. This child, only six years old, already has an international world view. But what about his peers in a high-poverty school only a block away? Would that same conversation ever occur? Rich brains have no geographic limits, so we must expand beyond the walls of our classrooms to help all students become connected to the bigger world.

To that end, keeping up with current events in terms of news and world geography is another way to replicate the quality learning experiences that more affluent sites provide. When I visit rich-brain schools, I see a very definite trend. They are connected to the world visually. I see the following in every site:

- Maps and globes in every classroom and clearly used daily. Bulletin boards, examples of pupil work, and ongoing projects are connected to these tools.

- There are current event boards or other graphic organizers that teachers use to inform and engage students with news and trends.

- Newspapers and other forms of media are part of the curriculum.

I started asking why globes and maps were not visible in many high-poverty schools that I visited, thinking that these tools were not available because of cost. I was wrong. Globes and maps were stashed in closets or behind curtains in storage or in the media center. Teachers simply were not using them routinely. There seemed to be a sense that "these students," the poor students, should be spending their time on the basics, not on frivolous things like finding their state capitol on a map or talking about an earthquake in China and locating it on the globe.

In what I now recall as a poignant and very teachable moment that was lost, second graders in a high-poverty site were writing friendly letters. The teacher was facilitating a pre-writing brainstorm, and one little boy said something like this: "My cousin is at the war. He is at the war in Iraq. He used to be at the war in Korea. I want to write him a letter at the war." He did a great job pronouncing the names of these foreign places. The other children were curious, and some also had family members also serving in harm's way. I was scripting the lesson and literally had to sit on my hands to keep from crawling under the curtained table where I knew a dusty globe sat unused. The teacher just kept going, talking about where to place the comma after the salutation.

In the wonderful children's book *The Year of Miss Agnes* that I use to model innovate teaching practices with my education students, Miss Agnes, who is teaching in a one-room schoolhouse near the Arctic Circle right after World War II, captures her students' attention by using maps to teach almost anything. The students express pride in knowing more about the world around them, and their confidence about learning in general seems to grow exponentially by using these tools. Like Miss Agnes, teachers in high-poverty sites can get a lot of value added to teaching by simply using maps, globes, and current events boards daily.

Career Planning as More Than a Dressed-Up Field Day

The final section on experiential learning turns our attention to career planning. It must be more than a once-a-year parade in which guests cycle through wearing uniforms or giving out corporate logo water bottles. Students who live in poverty need a long-range plan for leaving what is familiar and possible for what may seem unfamiliar and impossible. To that end, here are three strategies that I have observed in high-poverty sites that do a really good job of changing students' minds about their career paths:

1. College and university regalia are used not simply as decor in the school but as a tool for career planning.

2. Students are given learning styles and personality assessments routinely and talk about their skills and abilities with confidence. Visit www.educationinsite.com for a free kid's personality inventory.

3. Career planning is tied to academics. For example, when learning about the circulatory system, a cardiologist visits. When studying money, a bank teller comes in to do a presentation.

Whether our students are frisky four-year-olds or feisty fourteen-year-olds, the end game is to move them toward a path of independence and productivity. This translates to what we like to call *career readiness*. I think it is fair to say that rich-brain students are more often born career ready. They engage in life from a proactive, not reactive, posture. Their parents' educational backgrounds and exposure to highly successful adults in the workplace give them an edge and the confidence to go after what they want in life. We must teach that attitude to students who may believe that remaining reactive is a safer position in life and the only one that makes sense.

This is part of the "proactive, not reactive" thought process to be discussed in detail in chapter five. To help students develop this critical thinking skill set, be sure to:

- Implement career assessments and profiles as early as grade 5
- Set expectations for scholarly behavior, including the pursuit of scholarships
- Help students build life plans, not just career plans
- Teach practical skills that lead to independent living, such as money management, reading nutrition labels, and planning travel
- Create lessons that require independent work, think-pair-share, and cooperative group configurations that reflect the demands of a global workplace

Let's hear from two successful school leaders who have been implementing these skills.

Voices from the Field:
Lisa Hendricks

Executive Director of the Partnership Academy in Minneapolis, a unique K-5 charter school serving an exclusive Title I population. PA has a mission to "create learning experiences and partnerships that empower students to achieve their greatest potential in order to be positive contributors in their community."

"At our school, we are constantly looking for ways to partner with stakeholders within our community and find resources to further support learning in the classroom. For example, we sent out letters to almost every university, college, community college and tech school in the U.S. and asked them to send us a pennant from their school along with any other college gear that they would be willing to give us for our students. Almost every college we contacted sent us a pennant along with t-shirts, pencils and other fun gear from the school. We had volunteers help us get the letters mailed out along with a follow up thank-you note. We now have our students wear college gear as an alternative to their uniform on Fridays, and we have several college and university pennants hanging in the hallway as a way to reinforce that our students are intelligent and have what it takes to be college-bound. Additionally, our 4th and 5th grade students attend 2-3 college visits per year in order to further nurture the belief that they are intelligent and capable of attending college."

"Our students wear uniforms every day because we know that it's one of the ways to set them up for success and remind them that school is about business. It prompts them to remember that they are scholars who have an important job to do every day. We also believe it is important to take time to honor our students' cultural identities, so we have implemented College and Culture Fridays where students are able to wear college gear or any other type of clothing that represents and or showcases their cultures. This establishes a great sense of pride and belonging in each student and throughout the school community."

Voices from the Field:
Dr. Luci Carter

Dr. Carter has devoted 39 years to the field. She believes passionately in making the school experience challenging for all children.

"My school is not a Title I school based on the percentage of students receiving free or reduced lunch, yet we serve a large and growing population of the 'working poor.' Over the past five years, we have added nine Head Start classes of three- and four-year-old students and two additional classes of state funded four-year kindergarten. We have a great many children who need language enrichment and stimulation. So, as a school we try to provide each child with two field trips each school year. Our youngest children can't take field trips because of program regulations. In order to provide them with similar experiences, we bring programs to school each month. These programs bring opportunities to participate in drama, fantasy, art, and music. Children in all of our grades are able to practice audience skills, learn about music from around our world, see fairy tales acted out by theater groups and watch acrobats jump, twirl, and spin. By bringing programs to our school, everyone benefits! Although most of our students don't qualify for free or reduced lunch, their families are often struggling to make ends meet. Field trips away from school often cost as much as $10.00. The cost of admission added to the cost for the gas and driver's time adds up very quickly. Bringing field trips in the form of programs to the school benefits everyone."

Summary of Chapter Four's Big Ideas

- Students do best with experiential learning. The challenge is to provide rich, rigorous experiences in and from which to learn.
- Simply providing AP or honors courses is not enough. Students and families need to be introduced to and supported through what may be a new academic paradigm.
- Thinking globally means taking students out into the world as often as possible and bringing the world into the school as intentionally as possible.
- Wiring the brain for a career path that is wide open and exciting requires a specific set of experiences that begin early.
- Professional development for teachers and staff should provide opportunities to reflect upon and respond to overt and covert levels of bias that may impede experiential learning.

Chapter Five

LEAP Across the Gap with Attitude

The test of a first-rate intelligence is the ability to hold two opposed ideas in mind at the same time and still retain the ability to function. — F. Scott Fitzgerald

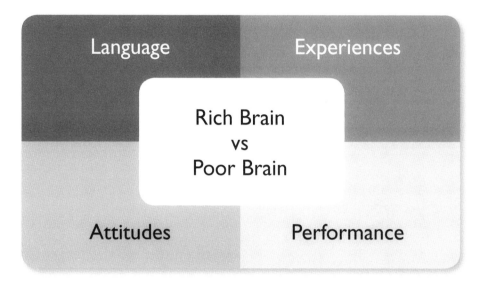

Language

Experiences

Rich Brain
vs
Poor Brain

Attitudes

Performance

One of the benefits of living in a more affluent home environment and subsequently attending a school that mirrors that environment is that you don't have to think about your future very much. The future is there before you, rosy and beckoning and probably rather attractive.

- You don't worry about a job. You ponder a career.

- You don't struggle to get to school every day. You think about the delightful events that will unfold when you walk onto the school grounds.

- Your attitude is positive, proactive and fueled by a belief that the world is at your feet lifting you up, not pulling you down.

- Attitude is everything. It makes us or breaks us. It is one of the four key elements that makes a brain rich or poor.

In affluent, highly successful schools, we see students engaging in:

- Critical thinking on a consistent basis, not as a rare challenge
- Debates and research across disciplines
- Projects and investigations that require a proactive, not reactive, mindset
- A student-centered constructivist approach

In contrast, less-challenging and typically less-wealthy schools provide a more ordinary, textbook-driven curriculum. Here we see students engaging in:

- Thinking at the first three (lower) levels of Bloom's Taxonomy
- Tasks such as answering questions or taking notes
- Teacher-centered instruction

Keep It Blooming

Bloom's Taxonomy lists six levels of thinking, ranging from simple to complex. The more complex the thinking, the richer the brain benefits. Moving students toward creating knowledge is the goal of a constructivist approach.

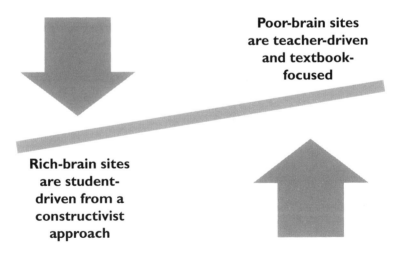

Poor-brain sites are teacher-driven and textbook-focused

Rich-brain sites are student-driven from a constructivist approach

In this chapter we will investigate the impact of the *affective domain*, that inner core of mind and spirit that shape our abilities to negotiate change, filter experiences, and respond to stimuli.

How can teachers, leaders, and parents whose sphere of influence is high-poverty, or poor-brain, schools inject a fresh new attitude? The three big ideas concerning attitudes that enrich brains and help replicate a more rich-brain experience for students are:

Confidence building through relationships

Proactive, not reactive, mindsets

A code of ethics

What does attitude have to do with the rich brain—poor brain disparity? Go back to our earlier discussions about fate and the accompanying risk of nihilism. Students from affluent backgrounds and schools can have problems, lots of problems. In fact, there is a backlash of sorts floating around social media and blogs in which folks are saying something like this:

> Rich students' parents are so busy making money and traveling and entertaining that they neglect them. Poor students' families may not have money, but at least they spend time with their children.

Every coin has two sides, no doubt, but the truth of the matter is this: money gives you choices. Having choices gives you hope. Therein sits the proverbial elephant in the schoolroom, if you will. Without choices, one becomes vulnerable to:

- Self-doubt
- Depression
- Anxiety
- Hopelessness
- Anger
- Impulsivity
- Sadness
- Helplessness

Strategy One: Confidence Building

Rationale

One of the most important tasks that sites serving poor students, or sites that serve large numbers of students who are not meeting potential, must undertake is developing the right attitudes among faculty and students. Affirming relationships are the first step.

Let's begin with the first big idea for chapter five – building brains and relationships through affirmations. I like to tackle affirmations through verbal and nonverbal behaviors. First, the non-verbal. Have you heard of mirror neurons?

Mirror neurons are nerve cells in the premotor cortex that respond when we perform an action and also when we see someone else perform that action. What does this matter to teachers in high-poverty sites? It has to do with two things that all students need and poor students often lack: empathy and trust.

> ## Mirror, Mirror in My Brain
>
> *Mirror neurons* are nerve cells in the premotor cortex that respond when we perform an action and also when we see someone else perform that action. What does this matter to teachers in high-poverty sites? It has to do with two things that all students need and poor students often lack: empathy and trust.

The mirror neuron system also appears to allow us to decode (receive and interpret) facial expressions. Whether we are observing a specific expression or making it ourselves (a frown of disgust, for example) the same regions of our brain become activated. And the better we are at interpreting facial expressions, the more active our mirror neuron system. These findings suggest that the mirror neuron system plays a key role in our ability to empathize and socialize with others, for we communicate our emotions mostly through facial expressions. (Society for Neuroscience)

Before we can help students whose brains are constantly assaulted by the stress hormone cortisol and whose immediate concerns are typically survival and fitting in to adopt a new set of attitudes, we must build a sense of empathy and trust. This means relationships.

One of the most important things I teach in workshops about the brain and stress is the importance of harnessing mirror neurons to build relationships. Ask yourself this question, no matter what kind of school you are attached to:

DO I GREET EVERY CHILD AT THE DOOR EVERY DAY, MAKING EYE CONTACT AND SENDING A POSITIVE AFFIRMATION?

Hear me on this: few things you can do are more important. Time and attention are at a premium in this world, and to build a rich brain, teachers must begin with fertile soil. The brain must be ready to absorb new ideas and take risks. Making eye contact, allowing mirror neurons to flash from human to human transmitting a code that says, "You are valuable. You are safe. You matter in this classroom. I am your advocate," will change the world one child at a time. As these mirror neurons do their magic, we prepare the brain for an influx of fresh ideas about what is possible. One of the more interesting studies I have encountered while doing this work suggests that students whose teachers mix things up in the classroom, who introduce good surprises in the instructional paradigm, trigger bursts of feel-good chemicals in the brain in a way that mimics opiates! Literally, a teacher can be a natural high. That is powerful.

Ask yourself, are you building relationships by creating a classroom environment that is surprising, engaging, and welcoming to all?

Surprise Feels Good to the Brain

Surprise plays a critical role in learning. Monkeys learn to recognize stimuli associated with rewards when those rewards came unpredictably. Keeping students primed for success allows the brain to function in a positive mode.

When the brain anticipates a reward and is looking for it, dopamine is fired. Dopamine brings feelings of pleasure. MRI scans of humans during a learning experience showed the pleasure center in the forebrain strongly activated by unpredictable stimuli. "The only other human study that activated the *nucleus accumbens* this much is one in which cocaine was injected," says Read Montague of the Baylor College of Medicine.

Building relationships through affirmative nonverbal and verbal exchanges is essential and does not cost a dime. It does require all of us who work with students and families to examine our own beliefs and intentions. Remember, mirror neurons do not lie and cannot be duped. We must believe in our students, and they must see, hear and feel those positive affirmations. In this "Voices from the Field," Dr. Ann Marie Watson, who has devoted her career to helping first-generation college students stay in and thrive in a college environment and who is herself a first-generation college success story, talks about the importance of 1) faculty building relationships at all grade levels, and 2) sending positive messages to students. She helps students build trust and establish *social capital*, the collective value of social networks.

Voices from the Field:
Dr. Ann Watson

Director of Student Support Services at Charleston Southern University

"In my office, the florescent overhead lights never need to be changed out; I never turn them on. Instead, in my personal 12' X 12' space you will find two standing lamps, two table lamps, and a desk lamp—glowing with soft white bulbs. I have a hand-me-down tapestry rug donated by my mother, pictures of my family (both two-legged and four-legged), various special mementos of my 25 years in higher education, a four-foot-tall wooden giraffe decorated with jewels (also from mom), a candy jar filled with goodies, and always a potpourri pot or candle warmer burning to fragrance the air with the various scents of the season."

"Intentionally, my office setting was designed to promote an environment that would both inspire and comfort me, through the countless hours of strategic planning, number crunching, and other problem- solving activities that are tacit to the role of a student services department head. It has served this purpose, as expected. What I did not anticipate was the reaction from almost every student who has been purposed to encounter my habitat. Invariably, as they are crunching on a Tootsie Pop (or some other goodie from the crystal jar) while seeking my insight into why their midterm grades include letters positioned beyond the letter C in the alphabet or my guidance for what major to choose, they will stop mid-sentence, release a sigh, and say something like 'Gosh, Dr. Watson, your office feels so homey, so relaxing.'"

"What I had intended solely for bringing solace unto myself also served to effect a seemingly powerful communication to the students I served... 'Come in, make yourself comfortable, talk with me.'"

"Oh, and I often get the same reaction from many of my colleagues (who also raid the candy jar, typically looking for something chocolate). When seeking to build relationships with others, be they peers or protégés, we should never underestimate the power of the subtle message to break down barriers – a smile, a comfortable chair, a candy jar…'"

Strategy Two: Attitude Adjustments

Rationale

Students need to adjust their brains to persist at tasks that seem difficult or to persevere in circumstances that seem unfair or unfixable. This requires a proactive instead of a reactive mindset.

It is not enough to tell students of any age that something is ok when it really isn't. Being authentic is absolutely essential if any of the LEAP ideas in this book can ever work. What we must learn to do, as we shape attitudes, is to help students figure out how to make it okay. I believe that the development of a proactive versus a reactive mindset is critical. You see, in a reactive state of mind, every event is a make-it-or-break-it situation. For example, doing poorly on a quiz is reason to shut down and give up on geometry. However, a proactive brain sees the big picture and can negotiate a poor grade as part of a pattern. The proactive brain thinks, "This is one grade, and, with some study time, it can be shored up by better grades." But this takes support. In affluent situations, students' brains have lots of support. That is what allows them to make mistakes and then get up and try again, to feel confident in taking creative risks, to imagine themselves doing bold and exciting things in life. We want to replicate that cognitive and metacognitive support. This strategy is the development of a proactive mindset.

There are three strategies that I find helpful in addition to the use of mirror neurons that we have already introduced. These are:

1. Active listening – the art of paying careful attention to what a student says, and then repeating it back to help clarify and dignify his or her words and ideas

2. Confirming support – the art of helping a student hold onto a belief that he or she is capable of doing the work necessary to succeed in a task

3. Redirecting negative thoughts – the art of helping a student get back on track with a purposeful plan by using affirming words and phrases

> ## Attitude is All Important
>
> It is not enough to tell students of any age that something is okay when it really isn't. Being authentic is absolutely essential if any of the LEAP ideas in this book can ever work. What we must learn to do as we shape attitudes is to help students figure out how to make it okay. That requires a proactive mindset.

These three strategies help shift brains from a reactive to a proactive position. Here is the desired paradigm:

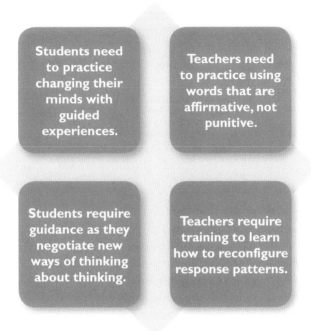

Students need to practice changing their minds with guided experiences.

Teachers need to practice using words that are affirmative, not punitive.

Students require guidance as they negotiate new ways of thinking about thinking.

Teachers require training to learn how to reconfigure response patterns.

Positive nonverbal and verbal affirmations help to shape rich-brain attitudes. In many cases, students need to practice new ways of thinking and speaking so that these attitudes become hard-wired. I suggest using anchor charts, teacher training, and *re-attribution training*, a therapeutic technique in which the client is encouraged to consider possible alternate causes for events.

In order to replicate the constant and consistent exposure to an attitude that says, "I can, and I will," teachers in high-poverty sites will need to fill students' ears with new words and fresh attitudes. The ubiquitous anchor chart is ideal for this replication. I would put charts in every classroom and in key gathering areas. I would also make it the theme of a Title I parent engagement session.

Moreover, I would not assume that teachers have been prepared to guide students through this kind of critical thinking. Most teachers learned these strategies in their own university education, if not before. They may not realize that many students have no clue about the possibility of changing words to change minds. A structured professional development opportunity aligned with additional training on active listening and cultural diversity is in order.

Finally, I believe teachers and leaders in high-poverty sites could benefit from a more expensive but valuable preparation in reattribution training. Students whose brains are constantly assaulted by cortisol have trouble shifting into the kind of critical thinking that allows one to examine cause and effect. They hunker down quickly into a life position that says, "I am bad and there is nothing I can do about it." Helping students to consider options for problems or setbacks and to not immediately seek blame or retreat into non-engagement is a tricky and technical skill set that takes a long time to perfect. As your site develops strategic plans for professional development, talk about the option of bringing someone in from a counseling center, or tap your school psychologist's repertoire to set up a training. I think it is worth the time.

Strategy Three: A Code of Ethics

Rationale

Living by a code is helpful and builds both personal integrity and group unity. What does your school's code say about attitude?

As we discuss the necessity of both a code of ethics and an embedded character education program in all sites, but especially those where students struggle for academic success, it is helpful to revisit the work of Dr. Annette Lareau, whose groundbreaking work on social inequities was discussed in chapter one. In February of 2015, the American Sociological Review published a piece examining the "rest of the story."

> Using both qualitative longitudinal data collected 20 years after the original Unequal Childhoods study and interview data from a study of upwardly mobile adults, this address demonstrates how cultural knowledge matters when white and African American young adults of differing class backgrounds navigate key institutions. I find that middle-class young adults had more knowledge than their working-class or poor counterparts of the "rules of the game" regarding how institutions worked. They also displayed more of a sense of entitlement to ask for help. When faced with a problem related to an institution, middle-class young adults frequently succeeded in getting their needs accommodated by the institution; working-class and poor young adults were less knowledgeable about and more frustrated by bureaucracies. This address also shows the crucial role of "cultural guides" who help upwardly mobile adults navigate institutions. While many studies of class reproduction have looked at key turning points, this address argues that "small moments" may be critical in setting the direction of life paths. (American Sociological Review, February 2015)

So often, what separates a child from failure and success is a small moment in time in which someone or something causes a shift in attitude. He or she changes course, changes a decision, changes a mindset and often because a voice reminds him or her that something better is possible.

Lareau's work mentions cultural guides that help rich brains, or what the study terms *upwardly mobile*, to find a way through or around stumbling blocks, all the while asking for help and responding to the (often unwritten) rules of the game. Thus, in this final piece of chapter five, let's help students by writing down the rules of the game in a classroom code of ethics.

What does a code of ethics look like? There are many, many ways to proceed here, but I would look at a few highly successful rich-brain schools and see what they expect from and for their students. Don't all students deserve the best?

I will provide a few essentials for a classroom code of ethics, but I should make something clear. I am not talking about a code of conduct or school rules. All of these things are helpful and have a place in the curriculum. I am going deeper here, into unchartered territory for many of us. This is the stuff of ivy halls and prestigious academies. I am taking all students to a different level. Let's get real and hands-on with codes that define things like:

Voices from the Field:
Dr. Andre Dukes

Principal of a rural high school serving a high-poverty community

"In my role as principal at a high-poverty, rural school, I have found that delivering solid academics is not enough. It is important to teach and model desired morals and ethics in schools because there seem to be gaps between the 'codes' of the neighborhoods and the 'codes' of the 21st century workplace. So, if we want students to transcend their neighborhood, we must give them the currency to do so."

"Delivering this essential currency, part academics and part ethics helps to make students citizens of the community, country, and world. Academics prepare students to understand the content, but ethics and values allow students to apply it. That application in context is a big part of my job. For example, politeness, active listening, and integrity open doors and encourage people from all cultural, social and geographic backgrounds to open up to you. Academics alone will not suffice."

"In the context of a competitive global economy, it is tough to succeed. The new global leaders will often have to work within a spider web of deceit and forge their own path of honesty and morality. They cannot be naïve nor unprepared. Teaching students how to lead ethically allows them to gain respect and move forward in society. I cannot say that my students are prepared for college and career unless I have helped them to develop a personal code of ethics that is as strong as the one provided at any school in the nation or in the world."

Summary of Chapter Five's Big Ideas

- All students need to feel safe and smart. Mirror neurons build relationships that are necessary for healthy brains and optimum learning.

- Students must learn to adjust their brains to persist at tasks that seem difficult or to persevere in circumstances that seem unfair or unfixable. Teachers can guide them through these tough affective territories.

- Changing your words can change your mind. Teachers must guide students in what may be new territory with affirming words.

- Teachers and students may benefit from formal reattribution training to practice changing attitudes and behaviors that may be standing in the way of progress.

- Success and failure can turn on a dime and often by responding to an unwritten set of rules. Giving students a code of ethics can help to facilitate the path to college and career.

Chapter Six

LEAP Across the Gap with Performance

I'm grateful to intelligent people. That doesn't mean educated. That doesn't mean intellectual. I mean really intelligent. What black old people used to call 'mother wit' means intelligence that you had in your mother's womb. That's what you rely on. You know what's right to do. – Maya Angelou

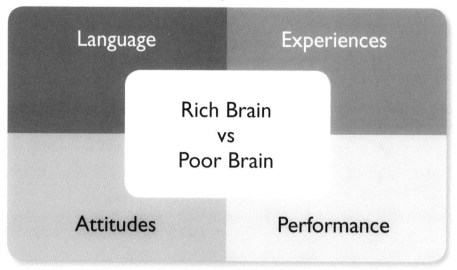

Language	Experiences

Rich Brain
vs
Poor Brain

Attitudes	Performance

"Mother wit" – innate, organic gifts that can be harnessed so that every brain might become a rich brain. This is the energy we will draw on to enhance intellectual and social performance. In chapter six, we will examine three Ws of performance that can help transform any school into a high-achieving site that serves all students well.

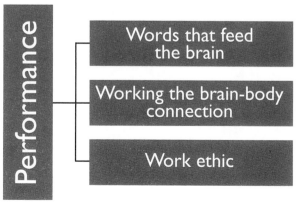

Performance

- Words that feed the brain
- Working the brain-body connection
- Work ethic

I'd like to establish my intentions toward *performance* in this context:

The action or process of carrying out or accomplishing an action, task, or function.

Performance is an action word. We want students to be able to independently and consistently perform tasks such as critical thinking, problem-solving, group projects, independent research, work completion, following directions, persevering through challenges, and contributing to the good of the group. These may seem like ordinary behaviors to expect from students and future workers, but they become daunting when a brain is operating under the threats described and outlined in the first few chapters of this book.

In affluent schools, performance is built into the program, with students routinely engaged in:

- Coaching and feedback across disciplines that enables what we call *growth praise*

- Long-term projects and team building

- Opportunities for team and individual sports, or well-equipped gyms and fitness classes to enhance brain-body connectivity

- Models and examples for work ethic that reject cultural and gender bias and reflect diversity

Teachers in high-poverty or average-performance sites must reconfigure their roles to teach and model the three Ws for rich-brain performance.

Words that feed the brain
Feedback and praise that are brain friendly, as defined by
Dr. Carol Dweck's model

Working the brain-body connection
The value of exercise to release stress and increase performance

Work ethic
Perseverance, persistence, performing day in and day out whether
you think you can or not

Where Do We Go Wrong?

A common error that seems to daunt many teachers who are trying very hard to challenge students with rigorous curriculum is the fact that they are not concurrently teaching the performance skills necessary for all students to engage with that kind of curriculum. Remember *mother wit*, that inborn intelligence that our students bring to the classroom? It is lovely, but it will burn out like a fire under glass if it is not nurtured and fed.

Again, we speak of the haves and have nots. For students who come from affluence and abundance, there is typically not one person, but an entire family, community, even legacy behind them fanning that fire. We must replicate experiences for our students who may not have the benefits at home or in their immediate community. There are many, many factors that contribute to performance. However, my goal is to showcase three big ideas that 1) have value added, 2) are valuable but do not cost a great deal, and 3) can be implemented at any site.

Performance is shaped by practice, experience, and feedback. It cannot simply be expected. It must be developed.

Words that Feed the Brain: Brain-Building Praise and Feedback

Rationale

Praise feels good, but the right kind of praise *does good* as well. Random praise is like a sugar high, a quick surge of feel-good chemicals followed by a crash. Brain-building praise is like protein, sustaining and building mass in the brain. Learn the difference, and see the differences in students.

If you haven't heard of Dr. Carol Dweck, you are missing a powerful opportunity to become a better teacher. I use her work to train future teachers and to enhance the work of practitioners. Dr. Dweck is one of the world's leading researchers in the field of motivation and is the Lewis and Virginia Eaton Professor of Psychology at Stanford University. Her research has focused on why people succeed and how to foster success. She says on her About the Author page at www.mindsetonline.com: "I have always been deeply moved by outstanding achievement and saddened by wasted potential."

In her ground-breaking 2007 article, Dweck explains how teachers are inadvertently holding students back:

> *I think educators commonly hold two beliefs that do just that. Many believe that (1) praising students' intelligence builds their confidence and motivation to learn, and (2) students' inherent intelligence is the major cause of their achievement in school. Our research has shown that the first belief is false and that the second can be harmful—even for the most competent students.* (Dweck, 2007)

How do we hold students back? We praise them for everything and thereby teach them nothing about what they did right or wrong, or well or poorly. Dweck says that there are risks associated with empty or "fixed" praise and benefits associated with "growth" praise.

> *Praise is intricately connected to how students view their intelligence. Some students believe that their intellectual ability is a fixed trait. They have a certain amount of intelligence, and that's that. Students with this fixed mindset become excessively concerned with how smart they are, seeking tasks that will prove their intelligence and avoiding ones that might not. The desire to learn takes a backseat.* (Dweck, 1999, 2006)

> *Other students believe that their intellectual ability is something they can develop through effort and education. They don't necessarily believe that anyone can become an Einstein or a Mozart, but they do understand that even Einstein and Mozart had to put in years of effort to become who they*

were. When students believe that they can develop their intelligence, they focus on doing just that. Not worrying about how smart they will appear, they take on challenges and stick to them. (Dweck, 1999, 2006)

Learning how to praise the right way is a first and critical step in building performance skills in all brains, but especially poor brains wired to give up quickly when things become dangerous and difficult in academic territory. I suggest professional development that targets the skill of giving *growth praise*, or praise that builds neuro-connectivity and real confidence in taking risks.

However, here is quick look at what I see as four important takeaways for sites that want to praise the right way:

Praise the
effort, not
the intellect

Keep praise
professional, not
personal

**Powerful
Praise**

Use dialogue
and questioning to
deliver praise and
feedback

Give specific
feedback about
effort

I suggest that sites consider the following strategies to implement a more robust and healthy praise and feedback climate that enhances student performance:

- Do a book or article study with other teachers using Dr. Dweck's work. Her webpage www.mindsetonline.com is a good place to start.

- Practice giving one another a feedback check by observing in the classroom and scripting lessons.

- Utilize those anchor charts. Post reminders about giving feedback prominently in the classroom so that students can help one another give healthy feedback.

Remember, all brains need to celebrate their ability to make choices from a position of free will, not from a deterministic mindset. This takes time and practice for both teachers and students. In closing this section, let's look at a quick switch from fixed to growth praise.

Fixed Brain Response	Growth Brain Switch	Your Thoughts
Good job	Tell me how you got that answer.	
Nice work	You used your spelling words in interesting ways. Try doing that again.	
Well done	I see that you followed the rules for that formula and found the right answer. How does that feel?	
Excellent	I am curious about your word choices. Tell me more.	

Feedback matters, whether in praise or using technology appropriately – another dilemma facing many schools. Using technology to stimulate creative and critical thinking is the topic from our next "Voice from the Field," Jack O'Connor.

Voices from the Field:
Jack O'Connor

*Assistant Title I Director, Montana Office of Public Instruction,
and former principal and teacher*

"The American school system, as a whole, seems to be caught in a difficult situation in balancing new technologies, new thinking, and the tried-and-true methodologies of the past. In my 25 years in education, 13 in the classroom, three as a principal, and nine at the state level, I see continuous swings in thought and application either to the far left or far right, but seldom do we find the desirable middle ground. This book offers a happy medium for Title I teachers who are trying to balance the direct instruction that research tells us works well with our students and the valuable engagement and instant feedback students enjoy using technology. So the question is, 'How do we meld the two together?'"

"First, teachers need to use technology to identify student academic weaknesses and establish baselines. Next, using direct instruction, our most highly qualified and effective teachers should work with our Title I students to improve academic achievement both in their daily work and missing skill set(s), especially those involving expressive language and critical thinking, skills for competitive workplace success. Then, technology can be used to reinforce learned skills and give feedback. Technology should be 'high touch,' not just 'high tech,' because our students need to be involved in relationships and language development all the time, not isolated with an iPad or laptop. Only by blending these two methodologies, 'high touch' and 'high tech,' together can we truly affect academic change for our Title I students."

The first step in enhancing performance as we LEAP across social and synaptic gaps is helping students develop healthy feedback loops, to be able to self-regulate their minds to move from a fatalistic to a futuristic point of view. The next step is to use the brain-body connection to its full advantage. Again, this is costless, but the benefits, like those of learning how to give and receive brain-building praise, are priceless!

Working the Brain-Body Connection

Rationale

Fit students have higher grades, better attention spans, and more opportunities to connect through sports and games that become the organic boardrooms of the adult world. We put less-affluent students at a disadvantage by ignoring the cognitive and social benefits of physical activity.

It starts earlier and earlier, losing the benefits of brain-body connections. In our well-meaning attempts to push students ahead academically, often with dull drill-and-kill lessons, equally valuable time for free play, recess, sports, physical activity, dance, running, roaming, and all sorts of beneficial movement is lost. Instead of pushing them ahead, we may be inadvertently pulling them away from critical neuro-connectivity made possible by the flow of glucose and oxygen to the brain that naturally stems from movement. Here's what the Washington Post said in the article *The Decline of Play in Preschoolers and the Rise in Sensory Issues:*

> *Preschool years are not only optimal for children to learn through play, but also a critical developmental period. If children are not given enough natural movement and play experiences, they start their academic careers with a disadvantage. They are more likely to be clumsy, have difficulty paying attention, trouble controlling their emotions, utilize poor problem-solving methods, and demonstrate difficulties with social interactions. We are consistently seeing sensory, motor, and cognitive issues pop up more and more in later childhood, partly because of inadequate opportunities to move and play at an early age.* (Strauss, 2015)

Fit brains are at an advantage. They are quicker, more curious, and more persistent. Research supports the regular and robust integration of physical and cognitive domains. Yet over and over we fail to make the connection. It pains me to say this, but every year in the late winter/early spring when schools begin to gear up to a maddening frenzy for standardized testing, we hear of principals, school boards, and panicked, competitive parents demanding that recess be cancelled until after the test is over. It is so sad and such a waste. Do they not know that there is something called *exercise-induced neurogenesis?*

- Movement connects neurons.

- Movement increases neurons.

- Movement helps boys to harness their preferred tactile-kinesthetic modality of learning.

- Movement allows girls to collaborate and plan in ways that they often prefer.
- Rats that run on an exercise wheel show 2-3 times the rate of *neurogenesis*, or birth of new neurons.
- Movement increases focus, an integral strategy in addressing ADHD.

Yes, it appears to be true. Movement can help modify the problematic behaviors of students who demonstrate the symptoms of ADHD, and we see a great many of these students in high-poverty sites. Why not take a closer look at the research?

In a new study from Michigan State University and the University of Vermont, research shows that offering daily before-school, aerobic activities to younger, at-risk children could help in reducing the symptoms of ADHD in the classroom and at home. Signs can include inattentiveness, moodiness and difficulty getting along with others. The study can be found in the *Journal of Abnormal Child Psychology, September 2014*.

"Early studies suggest that physical activity can have a positive effect on children who suffer from ADHD," said Alan Smith, chairperson of MSU's Department of Kinesiology, who conducted the research along with lead author Betsy Hoza, a psychologist from the University of Vermont.

There is a great deal of science involved in this discussion, but a few terms are worth spelling out. One term is BDNF, or *brain-derived neurotrophic factor*. One writer said that it is like Miracle Grow® for the brain. The benefits of BDNF are abundant. Dr. Darla Castelli and a team of scientists found that:

- Fit children allocate more brain activity to thinking.
- Fit children show more accuracy in thinking.
- Fit children used their brains more fluidly and effectively.

(Chaddock, Castelli, et al, 2013)

Working out the brain-body connection need not be expensive or fancy, but it must be accessible and available. Some strategies that make sense are provided in the table on the following page.

Option	Rationale	Your Notes
Cross country team or running club	• Inexpensive equipment • Builds stamina and work ethic	
Dance team or STEP club	• Integration of the arts • Boosts energy and focus	
Hikes in local parks and lessons outdoors	• Sunlight boosts creativity • Green spaces increase test scores	
Swimming lessons at local YMCA or college pool	• Water safety is important and often neglected	
Use free apps as brain breaks Examples include: • GoNoodle.com • JAM (Just a Minute) School Program • Super Stretch Yoga • Two-Minute Brain Breaks for the Elementary Classroom • JustbFit Classroom Energizers	• Boost circulation • Boost energy • Boost focus	
Use an inflatable beach ball with thinking prompts to toss as students move and answer	• Inexpensive • Simple • Cross-curricular	

Work Ethic

The third step in this section on performance is developing a strong and enduring work ethic. It is a traditional and even archaic sounding phrase, but let's revisit it from the point of view of cognitive and social science.

Rationale

It is a myth that poor students lack a work ethic. What seems to be true is that these students may not fully embrace the belief that a personal work ethic holds the power to help them reach goals or the ability to sustain that work ethic long enough to meet those goals.

It is important to note that the risk of unfairly stereotyping families is very high in this section. Poverty, as we discussed in the first chapters, is persistent and insidious and largely the result of inequities in educational opportunities and well-paid work. This quote from the Washington Post says it well:

> In fact, poor working adults work, on average, 2,500 hours per year, the rough equivalent of 1.2 full time jobs (Waldron, Roberts, & Reamer, 2004), often patching together several part-time jobs in order to support their families. People living in poverty who are working part-time are more likely than people from other socioeconomic conditions to be doing so involuntarily, despite seeking full-time work (Kim, 1999). (Strauss, 2013)

People are working very hard but at jobs that provide low levels of compensation, high levels of stress, exposure to toxins, and frustration. It is not more work, but a different, rich-brain work ethic that I want to encourage. What does that look like? We can start with some interesting research about financial wealth.

Motivational speaker Thomas C. Corely has studied this topic and written about it in a best-selling book. Although his focus is on acquiring financial wealth, and our intention is the acquisition of intellectual capital and emotional intelligence, there are many connections. I find his data set on habits to be useful in beginning this discussion of work ethic.

- 72% of the wealthy know their credit score vs. 5% of the poor
- 6% of the wealthy play the lottery vs. 77% of the poor
- 80% of the wealthy are focused on at least one goal vs. 12% of the poor
- 62% of the wealthy floss their teeth every day vs. 16% of the poor
- 21% of the wealthy are overweight by 30 pounds or more vs. 66% of the poor

- 63% of the wealthy spend less than one hour per day on recreational Internet use vs. 26% of the poor
- 83% of the wealthy attend/attended back-to-school night for their kids vs. 13% of the poor
- 29% of the wealthy had one or more children who made the honor roll vs. 4% of the poor
- 63% of wealthy listen to audio books during their commute vs. 5% of the poor
- 67% of the wealthy watch one hour or less of television per day vs. 23% of the poor
- 9% of the wealthy watch reality TV shows vs. 78% of the poor
- 73% of the wealthy were taught the 80/20 rule vs. 5% of the poor (live off 80%, save 20%)
- 79% of the wealthy network five hours or more per month vs. 16% of the poor
- 8% of the wealthy believe wealth comes from random good luck vs. 79% of the poor
- 79% of the wealthy believe they are responsible for their financial condition vs. 18% of the poor

(Corley, 2013)

We began this book talking about choices. I want to bring us back to that idea, giving students choices about how to channel their energies and commitments so that there is a greater intellectual and emotional return. This same idea was put forth in chapter five, with the growth praise mantra from Dr. Carol Dweck. Remember, ordinary praise provides a brief high of endorphins but leaves the brain running on empty, whereas growth praise is sustaining and nourishing to neural connections. Let's do the same with work ethic. Here I suggest three strategies that cost next to nothing, but provide positive returns:

1. Teach goal setting as a real topic.
2. Teach time management skills using multiple formats and doing daily planning benchmarks.
3. Teach students that there are rewards and consequences for completing or not completing tasks, and that they can control this cycle.

Work Ethic for Rich Brains

Much of what we will discuss in this final section of chapter six is acquired by experience among students who live in more affluent families. Skills such as managing a busy schedule, completing tasks on time, and following through on details are simply part of life when one has:

- All of the **tools** needed for success, such as a laptop, tablet, cell phone, and transportation to the library, tutors, or study groups

- All of the **time** needed for success, including a schedule typically free from an after-school job or caring for siblings

- All of the **support** needed to correct and redirect when a problem arises in problem solving, completing a task, or preparing for a test

Again, I draw on my own experience struggling to maintain a work ethic when I had other kinds of obligations. In high school, I wanted badly to run cross country and to be a part of the school yearbook staff as a copywriter. This was tough as I had responsibilities to care for my baby brother while my mom worked and my father was deployed in the military. With no transportation for these after-school activities, I took the bus home, picked up my baby brother from my mom so that she could go to a second-shift job, and then strapped my adorable sibling into a bicycle seat and rode several miles back to school for meetings or practice. It wasn't ideal, and at the time nobody quite knew what to do with this situation. I will never forget, however, the empathetic young running coach who began to bring his own toddler to practice for a play date with my baby brother. We would put a blanket and toys down in the grassy area of the track and let the little ones frolic while the team did laps. Coach never said a word – he just did it.

If we want to LEAP across social and synaptic gaps that separate students, teaching and modeling and nurturing a healthy work ethic that results in completing high school; completing a college or technical degree; or securing a position in an apprenticeship or in military service, steps must be taken. For each of the three big ideas, I will offer some targets.

Targets for Goal Setting Skills

- ✓ Teach terms such as *goals, objectives, timelines, assessment, review, task, steps, measurable,* and *achievable,* and use practical examples to explain.

- ✓ Set class and individual goals each week.

- ✓ Evaluate goals in terms of progress, not simply completion.

- ✓ Consider the importance of growth, not just success.

- ✓ Conference with students individually at least once per quarter.

- ✓ Use templates such as the one on the following page to help students visualize and track goals.

Getting to the Goal: My Weekly Organizer

Name_____ Date_____ Class_____

My goals for this week are:

1. _____

2. _____

These goals matter because:_____

_____

_____

_____

_____

_____

I will take the following steps to meet these goals:

Goal #1

1. _____ (Date Completed) _____

2. _____ (Date Completed) _____

3. _____ (Date Completed) _____

Goal #2

1. _____ (Date Completed) _____

2. _____ (Date Completed) _____

3. _____ (Date Completed) _____

Targets for Time Management Skills

✓ Teach and model terms such as *complete, deadline, progress, timeline, benchmark, planner,* and *agenda.*

✓ Encourage students to use an agenda or planner with a monthly view, and to color code by either subject or target. For example, use blue markers or stickers for study times, and use green markers or stickers for extracurricular practices. I realize that apps are all the rage, but truthfully, a page of big squares and the tangible experience of writing things down pleases the brain on many levels.

✓ Set up each class session with time for a good closure in which everyone pulls out agendas and updates goals and progress.

✓ Give students a learning styles assessment to help them pinpoint their strengths and weaknesses. You can try my free *Fruits of Learning for Kids* assessment, found at www.educationinsite.com.

✓ Show students how to look at time in blocks or chunks to be managed and measured.

Targets for Task Completion and Perseverance

✓ Reward small successes in completing tasks so that students learn how it feels to win.

✓ Use positive affirmations as discussed in chapter five, and post them around the classroom and school. Discuss them and analyze their potential for motivation.

✓ Familiarize yourself with Daniel Pink's model for motivation and apply it to students (check out the following page for details). Students need to know that there is a formula for success.

✓ Give feedback after task completion to help students develop the growth mindset discussed earlier.

✓ Share stories about men and women from similar social and cultural backgrounds as your students, and emphasize their willingness to simply put in the time rather than relying on luck or fate.

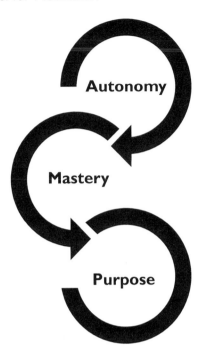

In his best-selling book *Drive: The Surprising Truth About What Motivates Us*, this self-help guru shares a trifecta for perseverance, and it is centered on motivation. We need to teach all students how to self-motivate, and this model is simple and accessible. In short:

1. Advance the concept of *autonomy*. Kids need to believe that it is within their power, and indeed their responsibility, to meet goals and complete tasks.

2. Emphasize the concept of *mastery*. Kids need to experience what it feels like to do academic tasks well and to be very good at something.

3. Discuss the power of *purpose*. Kids need to develop their own idea of what it means to do good, be good and feel good, and to connect these feelings to a higher purpose.

Dr. Rick Brewer, president of Louisiana College, knows what it means to work hard and to harness all three Ws described in chapter six. Let's hear from this "Voice from the Field."

Voices from the Field:
Dr. Rick Brewer

President of Louisiana College, musician, and educational leader

"I have worked with young people for three decades, as a college dean, in ministry, and raising two successful sons. In all these roles, I have discovered that the integration of these three Ws serves a pivotal role in leadership development. In fact, neglecting any of these traits leads to reduced productivity and minimal effectiveness. A daily commitment to practicing the three Ws alongside devotion to spiritual formation and faith development provides a positive framework for personal and professional success. Perseverance is the line of demarcation separating effective leaders from poor ones. If we want students to become successful, to have a real chance to fulfill their potential, we must be intentional about the three Ws, not leaving them to chance, but integrating them fully and modeling them with fidelity. At my inauguration as president of Louisiana College, I challenged those present to embrace the philosophy of 'And then some.' At one level, the 3 Ws can be viewed as an essential 'And then some' rule, the stuff of emotional intelligence that separates the ordinary from the extraordinary in schools and in life."

Summary of Chapter Six's Big Ideas

- Performance is shaped by practice, experience, and feedback. It cannot simply be expected. It must be developed.

- Certain kinds of feedback and praise encourage high levels of academic and personal performance, and other, more common ways of responding to students discourage those desired results.

- The brain-body connection is a valuable performance-building tool that is often underused. The attributes of BDNF are bountiful and accessible, but underemployed in schools.

- Work ethic cannot be underestimated and is often misunderstood and poorly presented and nurtured in schools. There are myths surrounding the topic of work ethic that should be considered to avoid unfair stereotyping.

- Professional development for teachers and staff should provide opportunities to learn how to give brain-friendly praise and feedback, to use physical activity to stimulate the brain-body connection, and to help students develop their own work ethics.

Chapter Seven

More Ideas and Innovations for Bridging Gaps

"Education," Horace Mann declared in 1848, *"is a great equalizer of the conditions of men, the balance wheel of the social machinery."*

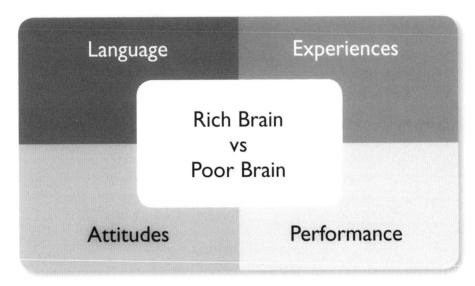

In chapters 3-6, we examined a cache of strategies specifically designed to LEAP across social and synaptic gaps in language, experiences, attitudes, and performance. In this final discussion, we will make a mad dash through the good things that I typically see in high-performing sites around the nation, no matter what their economic designation. Using the logic model on the following page, we will frame out a rationale for adopting these strategies to help children who live in poverty reduce cortisol levels in order to release metacognition and creativity.

The Logic Model

- Children who live in poverty need to use their most creative brains to find new pathways for learning and living.

- Children who live in poverty are subject to more cortisol, which impedes creativity.

- Therefore, we (teachers, leaders, parents) need to find creative ways to reduce cortisol and increase creativity.

Remember, a healthy brain can learn with relative ease, but a brain under the unique stressors that accompany poverty will freeze and downshift under the threat of the stress hormone cortisol and the concurrent impacts of poor nutrition, lack of sleep, and even lack of access to required medications for things like ear infections or dental problems.

The Challenge

Cortisol, the stress hormone, does so much damage to our brains as it seeps out: shutting down the pre-frontal cortex, impeding creativity; actually shrinking the hippocampus, the center of memory; and slowing neurogenesis. But when you recognize the fact that simply living in poverty triggers cortisol, even when there is no direct stressor like abuse or illness in a child's life, you have a huge problem.

Stress is a brain killer, and it can kill a student's desire to learn, ability to focus, and ability to retain information in long-term memory. These strategies are designed to diffuse the threats:

1. Integrate the arts across the curriculum.

2. Investigate a Montessori model.

3. Involve parents by building events that serve multiple purposes, such as a health screening combined with a speaker on healthy meals.

4. Initiate good relationships through home visits or by hosting events in community housing or local churches.

5. Inspire students by posting pupil work in prominent places around the building.

6. Invite families into the building with green spaces, water features, and attractive seating areas.

7. Improve the likelihood of family literacy by collaborating with bookmobiles, local libraries, national literacy events such as "Read for the Record," and by keeping the school library open extra hours and days.

Rationale

What do all seven of these big ideas have in common? They all work to connect neurons. For learning to occur in all sites, there must be a high and consistent level of neuro-connectivity. I even wrote a rhyme about it!

Neurons that wire together, fire together

Neurons that fire together, wire together

In adolescents, the experiences that they have will permanently affect the hard-wiring of the prefrontal cortex and sensitize the limbic system to cue in on feelings in a certain way. Every experience counts more in adolescence.

By wiring and firing neurons, new pathways are hard-wired for success. One hallmark of rich-brain schools is their commitment to wiring each child's brain to find its unique pathway, not to move "the herd roughly west'" as a professor of mine would say.

In the chart on the following page, we can see each of the seven strategies to reduce stress with some supporting ideas for implementation and room to jot down your ideas.

Key Ideas	Suggestions for Implementation	Value Added	Connect This To...	Your Notes
Integrate the arts	Art carts in every room (*more info available in *Brain Tips*, see next page)	• Addresses multiple intelligences	Holidays and seasonal celebrations	
Investigate a modified Montessori model	May be expensive, but can be modified	• Addresses the whole child more than a typical academic model	Head Start or Early Start initiatives	
Involve parents	Give door prizes such as baskets of "brain foods" (see next page)	• Builds trust and partnerships	PTA meetings and health screenings	
Initiate good relationships through home visits	Hold events in the meeting room of an apartment complex or in a local church if you cannot do each home visit	• Builds trust • Sends important messages	School nurses, pastors, and advocacy groups	
Inspire students by posting pupil work	Everywhere! (*more info available in *Brain Tips*, see next page)	• Raises healthy self-esteem • Motivates achievement	Partner with local artists' guilds to have them do framing as a donation	
Invite families into the building	Think green		Partner with local home improvement stores that offer grants to sites	
Improve the likelihood of family literacy	Book mobile - check out paperbacks and audio books for parents	• Raising parents' literacy moves students' literacy	Local literacy councils, the county library, offer GED on site	
Your Ideas?				

Resources

Brain Tips: Simple Yet Sensation Brain-Friendly Strategies for Improving Teaching, Learning, and Parenting is another resource of mine available from Lorenz Educational Press. I have pulled a few ideas from this text to use in our stress-reducing strategies:

- Art Carts – *Brain Tips*, page 58

  Art Carts are created with readily accessible art supplies including scented markers, glue sticks, glitter, wrapping paper and greeting card re-purposed items.

- Framing Student Work – *Brain Tips*, page 59

  Use elaborate, faux gold frames from the discount or dollar store to frame pupil work and display it. Students and parents love this!

- Suggested Brain Foods List:

  Almonds, green tea, raisins, blueberry muffin mix, cans of tuna or salmon, olive oil, dark chocolate, and peppermints.

More Ideas and Innovations for Bridging Gaps | 90/1135LE

Voices from the Field:
LaDene Conroy

Principal in Title I schools and Montessori advocate

"My heart is filled with boundless joy and tremendous passion for being first and always a teacher. I have taught children with differences, children with rich-brain and poor-brain backgrounds, as well as a variety of grades. I looped with my children and taught in multiage settings, always in a self-contained classroom. In my leadership role as a school principal, or 'the great teacher,' or the newest term 'lead learner,' I was sent in to change, shift and reconfigure very serious academic challenges and deteriorating settings and increase test scores. I have done this work for 34 years."

"I have been successful in turning around several schools that faced academic challenges, by following a protocol. The four steps include:

1. Providing an environment that has order through systems (procedures and routines provides structure and creates safe and clean learning landscapes);

2. Coordination in every aspect of the school day.

3. Developing learning environments that provide children with long, quiet learning periods in which to develop concentration for rigorous lessons.

4. Training teachers, children, and parents to independently follow the three steps naturally.

Within two months of school starting, while meeting with my teachers in small groups, the unanimous voice heard was – 'I can teach now and my children are learning.' 'The school is quiet and respectful.' 'There was a warm, cozy, and happy aura that was felt by guests and district officials as well as the staff and students.' 'I can't wait to come here each day.'"

"In recent years, I have become convinced that the Montessori Method is for all children, from all economic backgrounds. One unique aspect is The Peace Table or shelf, which is symbolic as well as an essential area in every Montessori environment. It is a place where students go to reconcile their differences using the peace rose and use their words when sharing their own feelings and confusions or learning to accept their school friends' differences."

"It is important to understand that Dr. Maria Montessori did not advocate that we teach the children about peace in the world. She directed us to create environments where children could experience the values that prepare them for adulthood in a way that would make them open to others' needs, values, and circumstances. Giving the children the skills to interact with others in a respectful manner as well as freedom and independence to develop following the laws of nature is the first step. In order for this to be possible, the educational system in the whole world needs to be re-evaluated and changed so that all children have these opportunities."

Voices from the Field:
Dr. Camacia Smith-Ross

Dean of the School of Education and Director of the Alternative Certification Program at Louisiana College, and former Director of Upward Bound, Title I Coordinator of Instruction, assistant principal, and classroom teacher

"Students' sense of value and self-worth are nurtured by their successes at a very early age, and teachers have the ability to grow and cultivate or stifle achievement in every child they teach. Although teaching is not an easy undertaking, it speaks to who you are as a professional. A teacher's input enhances the lives of students and radiates in student outcomes. Be proactive and share student successes by posting individualized and group work in conspicuous areas around the school building. This strategy validates ownership and cultivates intrinsic student pride."

"Likewise, school climate and culture nurture students' confidence and are enriched by both internal and external appearances. For families, school is an extension of the home or a safe haven away from home and should be attractive and inviting. Elements that can create inviting atmospheres are warm hues, scents, fountains, comfortable seating, plants, and lighting. Immediately acknowledging a parent or guardian's presence is a sign of respect and acceptance. Most importantly, remember to speak in a tone that is non-threatening and refreshing, making the school a welcoming place."

"Finally, as a former Title I Coordinator of Instruction, I find that family literacy encourages parents to initiate communication with teachers, learn about classroom-based literacy practices, and incorporate similar texts and activities within the home as an extension of the classroom. These practices strengthen and promote family involvement and support the work of the teacher. Family literacy initiatives should be fun and aligned to topics of interest. Every family member involved should enjoy it and be enlightened with a take-away, so that the home-school bond is strengthened."

Closing Remarks

It has never been more important to bridge social and synaptic gaps between schools. This is because more and more children are falling into these gaps. For the first time in a hundred years, the tacit rules for working hard and getting ahead are simply not working. Families are not getting ahead, and it hurts all of us.

Harvard political scientist Robert Putnam's new book, *Our Students: The American Dream in Crisis*, argues that the United States is losing its status as a land of opportunity for all. Here's the central idea: in the American Dream, upward mobility is available to all, limited only by ability and effort, not class. But Putnam assembles data to show that an "opportunity gap" has emerged here, making an upward climb much tougher in the 21st century compared with the mid-20th century.

Paychecks are getting smaller, even after the recession has retreated, if that is actually the case. Families are struggling. This is one outcome:

> Without steady factory paychecks, "there's such instability in the families of poor students that 60 to 70 percent of them — of all races — are living in single-parent families," Putnam said, versus 6 percent for the wealthiest fifth of families. Those students have fewer adults at the kitchen table, sharing conversation over dinner and pulling together. If you have two educated parents, "you'll have a larger vocabulary, you'll know more about the world," he said, and such children will have "a lot of adults in their life that are reaching out to help them. They tell them about what it means to go to college." (Putnam, 2015)

With families under attack and our culture trying to reconfigure the rules for getting ahead, it is often up to schools to find a remedy, or in the case here, a toolbox of remedies, to heal our academic wounds. Join me as we bridge the gaps, one book, one lesson, one teacher at a time.

References

Annie E. Casey Foundation. (2010). *EARLY WARNING! Why Reading By the End of Third Grade Matters.* Retrieved from http://www.aecf.org/resources/early-warning-why-reading-by-the-end-of-third-grade-matters

Berry-Hawes, J. (2015). *Left Behind: The unintended consequences of school choice.* Retrieved from http://data.postandcourier.com/school-choice/page/1

Center for Public Education. (2012). *Is High School Enough?* Retrieved from http://www.centerforpubliceducation.org/Main-Menu/Instruction/Is-high-school-tough-enough-At-a-glance/Is-high-school-tough-enough-Full-report.html

Chaddock, L., Erickson, K.I., Voss, M.W., Kencht, A.M., Pontifex, M.B., Castelli, D.M., Hillman, C.H., & Kramer, A. (2013). *The effects of physical activity on functional MRI activation associated with cognitive control in children: A randomized controlled intervention.* Frontiers in Human Neuroscience, 7(72). DOI: 10.3389/fnhum.2013.00072.

Conroy, P. (1972). *The Water is Wide.* New York: Dial Press.

Corley, T. (2013). *Will your child be rich or poor? 15 poverty habits parents teach their children.* Retrieved from http://richhabits.net/will-your-child-be-rich-or-poor/

Covey, S. (1989). *The 7 Habits of Highly Effective People: Powerful Lessons in Personal Change.* New York: Simon & Schuster.

Dweck, C. S. (1999). *Self-theories: Their role in motivation, personality and development.* Philadelphia: Taylor and Francis/Psychology Press.

Dweck, C. S. (2006). *Mindset: The new psychology of success.* New York: Random House.

Dweck, C. (2007). *The perils and promises of praise.* ASCD Journal, 65(2), 34-39.

Frederiksen, L. (2009). *Dr Volkow Leads 8-year Study – New ADHD Research Findings.* Retrieved from http://www.breakingthecycles.com/blog/2009/09/22/dr-volkow-leads-8-year-study-new-adhd-research-findings/

Geewax, M. (2015). *The Numbers Add Up To This: Less And Less Opportunity For Poor Kids.* Retrieved from http://www.npr.org/2015/03/10/391922654/the-numbers-add-up-to-this-less-and-less-opportunity-for-poor-students

Gentile, E. & Imberman, S. (2010). *Dressed for Success: The Effect of School Uniforms on Student Achievement and Behavior.* Retrieved from https://www.utdallas.edu/research/tsp-erc/pdf/seminar_paper_imberman.pdf

Gopnik, A. (2015) *Brains, Schools and a Vicious Cycle of Poverty.* Retrieved from http://www.wsj.com/articles/brains-schools-and-a-vicious-cycle-of-poverty-1431529998

Hair, N.L., Hanson, J.L., Wolfe, B.L., and Pollak, S.D. (2015). *Association of Child Poverty, Brain Development, and Academic Achievement.* Retrieved from http://archpedi.jamanetwork.com/article.aspx?articleid=2381542

Hart, B. and Ridley, T. (2003). *The Early Catastrophe: The 30 Million Word Gap by Age 3.* Retrieved from http://www.aft.org//sites/default/files/periodicals/TheEarlyCatastrophe.pdf

Hill, K. (2002). *The Year of Miss Agnes.* New York: Aladdin Books.

Karges-Bone, L. (2003). *Teachers: Doing Brain Surgery from the Inside Out.* Journal of Early Education and Family Review.

Karges-Bone, L. (2010). *Differentiated Pathways of the Brain.* Dayton: Lorenz Educational Press.

Karges-Bone, L. (2014). *Brain Tips: Simple Yet Sensational Strategies for Improving Teaching, Learning, and Parenting.* Dayton: Lorenz Educational Press.

Lareau, A. (2003). *Unequal Childhoods: Class, Race, and Family Life.* Berkeley: University of California Press.

Lareau, A. (2015). *Cultural knowledge and social inequality.* American Sociological Review, 80(1). Retrieved from http://asr.sagepub.com/content/80/1/1.abstract

Michigan State University. *Exercise before school may reduce ADHD symptoms in kids.* ScienceDaily. ScienceDaily, 9 September 2014. Retrieved from www.sciencedaily.com/releases/2014/09/140909093701.htm.

National Center for Education Statistics. (2015). *Children Living in Poverty.* Retrieved from https://nces.ed.gov/programs/coe/indicator_cce.asp

Nelson, E. (2014). *Abuse Casts a Long Shadow by Changing Children's Genes.* Retrieved from http://www.pbs.org/wgbh/nova/next/body/epigenetics-abuse/

Payne, R. (1996). *A Framework for Understanding Poverty.* Highlands, TX: aha! Process, Inc.

Perry, S. (2008). *Mirror Neurons.* Retrieved from http://www.brainfacts.org/brain-basics/neuroanatomy/articles/2008/mirror-neurons/

Pillars, W. (2011). *Teachers as Brain-Changers: Neuroscience and Learning.* Retrieved from http://www.edweek.org/tm/articles/2011/12/20/tln_pillars.html

Pink, D. (2011). *Drive: The Surprising Truth About What Motivates Us.* New York: Riverhead Books.

Putnam, R. (2001). *Bowling Alone: The Collapse and Revival of American Community.* New York: Simon & Schuster.

Putnam, R. (2015). *Our Students: The American Dream in Crisis.* New York: Simon & Schuster.

Rosenthal, R., & Fode, K. (1963). *The effect of experimenter bias on performance of the albino rat.* Behavioral Science, 8, 183-189.

Rosenthal, R., &. Jacobson, L. (1963). *Teachers' expectancies: Determinants of pupils' IQ gains.* Psychological Reports, 19, 115-118.

Scott, A. (2015). *The changing role of advanced placement classes.* Retrieved from http://www.marketplace.org/topics/education/learning-curve/changing-role-advanced-placement-classes

Strauss, V. (2013). *Five stereotypes about poor families and education.* Retrieved from https://www.washingtonpost.com/blogs/answer-sheet/wp/2013/10/28/five-stereotypes-about-poor-families-and-education/

Strauss, V. (2015). *The decline of play in preschoolers and the rise in sensory issues.* Retrieved from https://www.washingtonpost.com/blogs/answer-sheet/wp/2015/09/01/the-decline-of-play-in-preschoolers-and-the-rise-in-sensory-issues/

USDA Economic Research Service. (2015). *Persistent Child Poverty Counties, 2015.* Retrieved from http://www.ers.usda.gov/media/1842836/persistentchildpoverty2015fw.png

Volkow, N., et al. (2009). *Evaluating Dopamine Reward Pathway in ADHD.* Retrieved from http://jama.jamanetwork.com/article.aspx?articleid=184547

Whitehurst, J., and Lonigan, C. (1998). *Child Development and Emergent Literacy.* Child Development, 69(3), 848-872.